1st International Workshop on Automatic Translation for Signed and Spoken Languages 2021

Held at MT Summit 2021

Online
16 – 20 August 2021

ISBN: 978-1-7138-3921-7

Printed from e-media with permission by:

Curran Associates, Inc.
57 Morehouse Lane
Red Hook, NY 12571

Some format issues inherent in the e-media version may also appear in this print version.

Printed with permission by Curran Associates, Inc. (2022)

For permission requests, please contact the Association for Computational Linguistics at the address below.

Association for Computational Linguistics
209 N. Eighth Street
Stroudsburg, Pennsylvania 18360

Phone: 1-570-476-8006
Fax: 1-570-476-0860

acl@aclweb.org

Additional copies of this publication are available from:

Curran Associates, Inc.
57 Morehouse Lane
Red Hook, NY 12571 USA
Phone: 845-758-0400
Fax: 845-758-2633
Email: curran@proceedings.com
Web: www.proceedings.com

MT SUMMIT VIRTUAL 2021

Proceedings of Machine Translation Summit XVIII

https://mtsummit2021.amtaweb.org

1st International Workshop on Automatic Translation for Signed and Spoken Languages

Organizer: Dimitar Shterionov

Proceedings of the 1st International Workshop on Automatic Translation for Sign and Spoken Languages

Dimitar Shterionov d.shterionov@tilburguniversity.edu
Department of Cognitive Science and Artificial Intelligence, Tilburg University, Netherlands

1 Aim of the Workshop

According to the World Federation of the Deaf (WFD) over 70 million people are deaf and communicate primarily via a sign language (SL). Contrary to popular belief, SLs differ from spoken languages; they are not merely mappings of words in a spoken language into hand gestures. SLs are independent natural languages expressed in the visual-gestural modality with their own words and grammar that are separate from their regional spoken counterpart (Camgoz et al., 2018; Stokoe Jr, 2005). With more than 150 different sign languages[1] and more than 7000 spoken languages[2] crossing the signed-spoken language barrier in current times of increased globalisation and information flow is a challenging task, but one that is crucial for fair access of information.

Currently, human interpreters are the main medium for signed-to-spoken, spoken-to-signed and signed-to-signed language translation. The availability and cost of these professionals is often a limiting factor in communication between signers and non-signers. Machine translation (MT) is a core technique for reducing language barriers [for spoken languages]. Although MT has come a long way since its inception in the 1950s, it still has a long way to go to successfully cater to all communication needs and users. When it comes to the deaf community, MT is in its infancy.

The rapid technological and methodological advances in deep learning (DL), and in AI in general, that we have seen in the last decade, have not only improved MT, the recognition of image, video and audio signals, as well as the understanding of language, and the synthesis of life-like 3D avatars, etc., but have also led to the fusion of interdisciplinary research innovations that lays the foundation of automated translation services between signed and spoken languages. However, these recent advances have not yet improved the translation between signed and spoken, and between signed and signed languages to the extent of spoken-to-spoken MT where reaching human-level translation quality has been claimed more than once in the last 5 years (Junczys-Dowmunt et al., 2016; Wu et al., 2016; Hassan et al., 2018). Furthermore, lessons learned from research and development in the field of Natural Language Processing (NLP) (related to spoken language) have not yet been taken into account in the work of signed language researchers (Yin et al., 2021).

[1]The Ethnologue website (`https://www.ethnologue.com/subgroups/sign-language`) lists 150 sign languages; WFD reports more than 200 sign languages; other sources report up to 300 sign languages (e.g. `https://www.k-international.com/blog/different-types-of-sign-language-around-the-world/`).

[2]See `https://www.ethnologue.com/guides/how-many-languages` for an overview.

The goal of the first edition of the workshop on Automatic Translation for Signed and Spoken Languages (AT4SSL) is to reduce the aforementioned gaps in research and development of tool, techniques and methodologies for the automatic translation between signed and spoken languages. It provides a venue where researchers, practitioners, interpreters and innovators who focus on sign language linguistics, MT, NLP, interpreting of signed and spoken languages, image and video recognition (for the purpose of sign language recognition), 3D avatar and virtual signers synthesis, and other related fields can present complete or ongoing research and discuss problems, challenges and opportunities for the automated translation of signed-to-spoken, spoken-to-signed and signed-to-signed communication. The AT4SSL workshop encapsulates: (i) 8 long papers, presenting complete work; (ii) 3 short papers, presenting ongoing research; (iii) a key-note presentation and (iv) a panel discussion.

The work presented in this and other workshops[3] along with the increased financial support for large-scale projects working on signed and spoken language translation such as SignON (`https://signon-project.eu/`) and EASIER (`https://www.project-easier.eu/`) are indicative for the realisation that such a complex task needs to be addressed from different sides and through a multidisciplinary collaboration. As a workshop within the Machine Translation Summit 2021 (MTSummit 2021), the AT4SSL workshop also aims to bring closer the wider MT and the signed language research and development communities.

2 Paper Overview

The first edition of the AT4SSL workshop received 15 submissions (including long and short papers). Eight long papers, presenting completed work, and three short papers, presenting ongoing work were accepted to be presented at the workshop.

Three long papers present work on translation of sign language (gloss or video) into text, exploiting existing and proposing new techniques based on low-resource MT approaches. These papers are:[4]

- "Frozen Pretrained Transformers for Neural Sign Language Translation" (long paper) by Mathieu De Coster, Karel D'Oosterlinck, Marija Pizurica, Paloma Rabaey, Severine Verlinden, Mieke Van Herreweghe and Joni Dambre
- "Data Augmentation for Sign Language Gloss Translation" (long paper) by Amit Moryossef, Kayo Yin, Graham Neubig and Yoav Goldberg
- "Approaching Sign Language Gloss Translation as a Low-Resource Machine Translation Task" (long paper) by Xuan Zhang and Kevin Duh.

Two position papers discuss specific pitfalls, challenges and ethical considerations in the development of sign language technologies with a more in-depth focus on 3D avatars. These are:

- "The Myth of Signing Avatars" (long paper) by Rosalee Wolfe, John C. McDonald, Eleni Efthimiou, Evita Fontinea, Frankie Picron, Davy Van Landuyt, Tina Sioen, Annelies Braffort, Michael Filhol, Sarah Ebling, Thomas Hanke and Verena Krausneker
- "Is "good enough" good enough? Ethical and responsible development of sign language technologies" (long paper) by Maartje De Meulder

[3]For example, the workshop on Sign Language Translation and Avatar Technologies (SLTAT) `http://sltat.cs.depaul.edu/` and the workshop on Sign Language Recognition, Translation and Production (SLRTP) `https://slrtp.com/`.

[4]Following alphabetic order based on the author's surname.

One long paper and one short paper present work on synthesis of sign language, i.e. text-to-sign and 3D avatar synthesis on AR glasses:

- "AVASAG: A German Sign Language Translation System for Public Services" (short paper) by Fabrizio Nunnari, Judith Bauerdiek, Lucas Bernhard, Cristina España-Bonet, Corinna Jäger, Amelie Unger, Kristoffer Waldow, Sonja Wecker, Elisabeth André, Stephan Busemann, Christian Dold, Arnulph Fuhrmann, Patrick Gebhard, Yasser Hamidullah, Marcel Hauck, Yvonne Kossel, Martin Misiak, Dieter Wallach and Alexander Stricker

- "Automatic generation of a 3D sign language avatar on AR glasses given 2D videos of human signers" (long paper) by Lan Thao Nguyen, Florian Schicktanz, Aeneas Stankowski and Eleftherios Avramidis

Two long and two short papers address other miscellaneous topics:

- "Sign and Search: Sign Search Functionality for Sign Language Lexica" (long paper) by Manolis Fragkiadakis and Peter van der Putten – which presents different methods for search and retrieval of signs from sign language lexica using OpenPose keypoints.

- "Using Computer Vision to Analyze Non-manual Marking of Questions in KRSL" (long paper) by Anna Kuznetsova, Alfarabi Imashev, Medet Mukushev, Anara Sandygulova and Vadim Kimmelman – which a manual and an automatic analysis of non-manual markings in Kazakh-Russian Sign Language (KRSL) as presented in yes/no and wh- questions. The automated analysis uses an approach based on OpenPose.

- "Online Evaluation of Text-to-sign Translation by Deaf End Users: Some Methodological Recommendations" (short paper) by Floris Roelofsen, Lyke Esselink, Shani Mende-Gillings, Maartje de Meulder, Nienke Sijm and Anika Smeijers

- "Defining meaningful units. Challenges in sign segmentation and segment-meaning mapping" (short paper) by Mirella De Sisto, Dimitar Shterionov, Irene Murtagh, Myriam Vermeerbergen and Lorraine Leeson – the only linguistically oriented paper which discusses challenges related to mapping signs into meaning units that can allow the processing of sign language with established NLP and MT tools and techniques.

3 Invited Speakers

This first edition of the AT4SSL hosts one invited talk and a panel discussion. The key-note speaker is:

Prof Lorraine Leeson (key-note) (female) holds a Dip. Deaf Studies (interpreting), M.Phil Linguistics, PhD. Linguistics. Cert. Gender Studies. She is Professor in Deaf Studies at the Centre for Deaf Studies, School of Linguistics, Speech and Communication Sciences and Associate Dean of Research (Research Integrity) for Trinity College Dublin (2018-present). Prof Leeson has worked with Deaf communities in a range of capacities since 1990. She served as inaugural Director of the Centre for Deaf Studies at Trinity College Dublin from 2001-17. Her research work is multidisciplinary in nature. Her doctoral work was the first to examine aspects of the morphosyntax of Irish Sign Language, and subsequent to this, she has published widely on aspects of the grammar of Irish Sign Language, as well as on applied linguistics topics, including a significant body of work on sign language interpreting (16 books, 58 papers, 13 edited volumes (journals/monographs) and 100+ peer-reviewed conference papers). She was named a European Commission European Language Ambassador for her work on sign languages in 2008. Lorraine was a member of the first cohort of professionally trained Irish Sign Language/English interpreters in Ireland, and she continues to interpret. She has engaged in pan-European research work with academic institutions, Deaf communities and interpreting organisations since 1990, serving as Chair of the European Forum of Sign Language Interpreters Committee of Experts (2013-2019). She is a member of the Royal Irish Academy's Committee on Languages, Literatures and Cultures (LLC) (2018-present).

The panel will feature seven prominent experts in the fields of machine translation, machine learning, engineering, sign language linguistics and computational linguistics, data collection and processing (for the purposes of sign language research) and avatar and 3D technologies. The panel members are:

- **Mr Mark Wheatley**, Executive Director of the European Union of the Deaf (EUD), Belgium
- **Prof Gorka Labaka**, Assistant professor at the Engineering School of the University of the Basque Country (UPV/EHU), Spain
- **Prof Christian Rathmann**, Professor in Deaf Studies Interpreting at Humboldt University, Germany.
- **Dr Sarah Ebling**, Lecturer and research associate at the University of Zurich and the University of Applied Sciences of Special Needs Education Zurich (HfH), Switzerland.
- **Prof Myriam Vermeerbergen**, Associate Professor at KU Leuven, Belgium
- **Mr Thomas Hanke**, Research Associate at the University of Hamburg, Germany.
- **Prof Richard Bowden**, Professor of Computer Vision and Machine Learning at the University of Surrey, the UK.

4 Committees

4.1 Organisation committee

- Dimitar Shterionov (workshop chair), Tilburg University
- Carmel Grehan, Trinity College Dublin
- Mathieu De Coster, Ghent University
- Aoife Brady, The ADAPT Centre, Dublin City University
- Davy Van Landuyt, European Union of the Deaf
- Jorn Rijckaert, Vlaams GebarentaalCentrum,
- Catia Cucchiarini, Dutch Language Union (Nederlandse Taalunie)
- Mirella De Sisto, Tilburg University
- Vincent Vandeghinste, KULeuven / Instituut voor de Nederlandse Taal

4.2 Program committee

- Abraham Glasser, Rochester Institute of Technology
- Ahmet Alp Kindiroglu, Bogazici University
- Amanda Duarte, Barcelona Supercomputing Center

- Amit Moryossef, Bar-Ilan University, Google
- Daniel Stein, eBay Inc.
- Eva Vanmassenhove, Tilburg University
- Frédéric Blain, University of Wolverhampton
- Iacer Calixto, University of Amsterdam
- Ineke Schuurman, KU Leuven
- Ioannis Tsochantaridis, Google
- Kayo Yin, Carnegie Mellon University
- Maartje De Meulder, University of Applied Sciences Utrecht
- Rosalee J. Wolfe, ILSP / Athena RC
- Tsourakis Nikos, University of Geneva

Acknowledgements

This workshop has been organised within the framework of the SignON project. This project has received funding from the European Union's Horizon 2020 research and innovation programme under grant agreement No 101017255.

References

Camgoz, N. C., Hadfield, S., Koller, O., Ney, H., and Bowden, R. (2018). Neural sign language translation. In *Proceedings of the IEEE Conference on Computer Vision and Pattern Recognition*, pages 7784–7793.

Hassan, H., Aue, A., Chen, C., Chowdhary, V., Clark, J., Federmann, C., Huang, X., Junczys-Dowmunt, M., Lewis, W., Li, M., et al. (2018). Achieving human parity on automatic chinese to english news translation. *arXiv preprint arXiv:1803.05567.*

Junczys-Dowmunt, M., Dwojak, T., and Hoang, H. (2016). Is neural machine translation ready for deployment? *Proceedings of the 13th International Workshop on Spoken Language Translation (IWSLT 2016)*, 30.

Stokoe Jr, W. C. (2005). Sign language structure: An outline of the visual communication systems of the american deaf. *Journal of deaf studies and deaf education*, 10(1):3–37.

Wu, Y., Schuster, M., Chen, Z., Le, Q. V., Norouzi, M., Macherey, W., Krikun, M., Cao, Y., Gao, Q., Macherey, K., Klingner, J., Shah, A., Johnson, M., Liu, X., Kaiser, L., Gouws, S., Kato, Y., Kudo, T., Kazawa, H., Stevens, K., Kurian, G., Patil, N., Wang, W., Young, C., Smith, J., Riesa, J., Rudnick, A., Vinyals, O., Corrado, G., Hughes, M., and Dean, J. (2016). Google's neural machine translation system: Bridging the gap between human and machine translation. *CoRR*, abs/1609.08144.

Yin, K., Moryossef, A., Hochgesang, J., Goldberg, Y., and Alikhani, M. (2021). Including Signed Languages in Natural Language Processing. *arXiv:2105.05222 [cs].* arXiv: 2105.05222.

Contents

Data Augmentation for Sign Language Gloss Translation

Amit Moryossef amitmoryossef@gmail.com
Bar-Ilan University

Kayo Yin kayoy@cs.cmu.edu
Language Technologies Institute, Carnegie Mellon University

Graham Neubig gneubig@cs.cmu.edu
Language Technologies Institute, Carnegie Mellon University

Yoav Goldberg yogo@cs.biu.ac.il
Bar-Ilan University, Allen Institute for AI

Abstract

Sign language translation (SLT) is often decomposed into *video-to-gloss* recognition and *gloss-to-text* translation, where a gloss is a sequence of transcribed spoken-language words in the order in which they are signed. We focus here on gloss-to-text translation, which we treat as a low-resource neural machine translation (NMT) problem. However, unlike traditional low-resource NMT, gloss-to-text translation differs because gloss-text pairs often have a higher lexical overlap and lower syntactic overlap than pairs of spoken languages. We exploit this lexical overlap and handle syntactic divergence by proposing two rule-based heuristics that generate pseudo-parallel gloss-text pairs from monolingual spoken language text. By pre-training on this synthetic data, we improve translation from American Sign Language (ASL) to English and German Sign Language (DGS) to German by up to 3.14 and 2.20 BLEU, respectively.

1 Introduction

Sign language is the most natural mode of communication for the Deaf. However, in a predominantly hearing society, they often resort to lip-reading, text-based communication, or closed-captioning to interact with others. Sign language translation (SLT) is an important research area that aims to improve communication between signers and non-signers while allowing each party to use their preferred language. SLT consists of translating a sign language (SL) video into a spoken language (SpL) text, and current approaches often decompose this task into two steps: (1) *video-to-gloss*, or continuous sign language recognition (CSLR) (Cui et al., 2017; Camgoz et al., 2018); (2) *gloss-to-text*, which is a text-to-text machine translation (MT) task (Camgoz et al., 2018; Yin and Read, 2020b).

In this paper, we focus on gloss-to-text translation. SL data and resources are often scarce, or nonexistent (§2; Bragg et al. (2019)). Gloss-to-text translation is, therefore, an example of an extremely low-resource MT task. However, while there is extensive literature on low-resource MT between spoken languages (Sennrich et al., 2016a; Zoph et al., 2016; Xia et al., 2019; Zhou et al., 2019), the dissimilarity between sign and spoken languages calls for novel methods. Specifically, as SL glosses borrow the lexical elements from their ambient spoken language, handling syntax and morphology poses greater challenges than lexeme translation (§3).

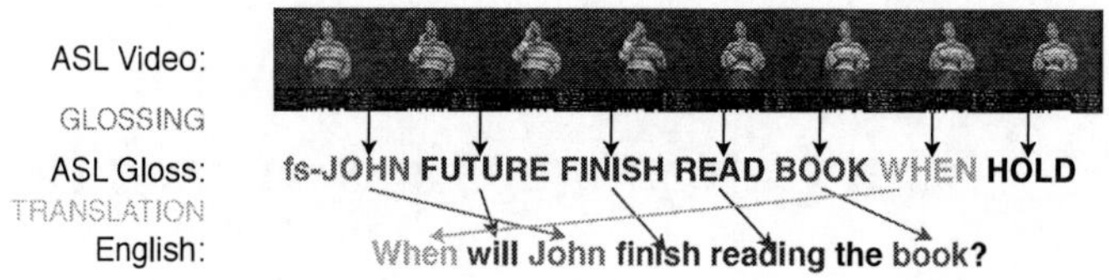

(a) ASL video with gloss annotation and English translation

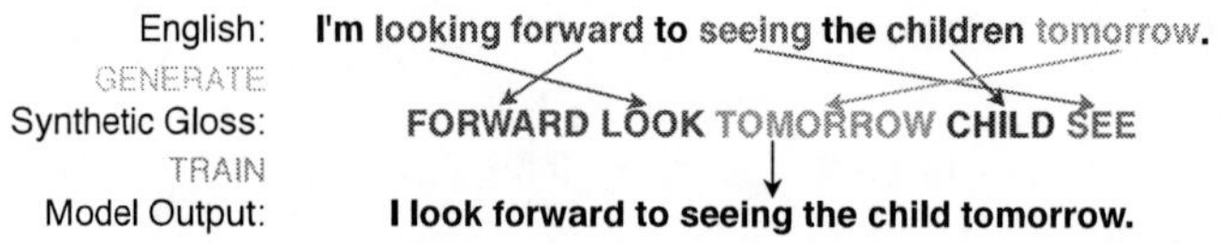

(b) Data augmentation and training

Figure 1: Real and synthetic gloss-spoken pairs.

In this work, we (1) discuss the scarcity of SL data and quantify how the relationship between a sign and spoken language pair is different from a pair of two spoken languages; (2) show that the *de facto* method for data augmentation using back-translation is not viable in extremely low-resource SLT; (3) propose two rule-based heuristics that exploit the lexical overlap and handles the syntactic divergence between sign and spoken language, to synthesize pseudo-parallel gloss/text examples (Figure 1b); (4) demonstrate the effectiveness of our methods on two sign-to-spoken language pairs.

2 Background

Sign Language Glossing SLs are often transcribed word-for-word using a spoken language through *glossing* to aid in language learning, or automatic sign language processing (Ormel et al., 2010). While many SL glosses are words from the ambient spoken language, glossing preserves SL's original syntactic structure and therefore differs from translation (Figure 1a).

Data Scarcity While standard machine translation architectures such as the Transformer (Vaswani et al., 2017) achieve reasonable performance on gloss-to-text datasets (Yin and Read, 2020a; Camgoz et al., 2020), parallel SL and spoken language corpora, especially those with gloss annotations, are usually far more scarce when compared with parallel corpora that exist between many spoken languages (Table 1).

	Language Pair	# Parallel Gloss-Text Pairs	Vocabulary Size (Gloss / Spoken)
Signum (von Agris and Kraiss, 2007)	DGS-German	780	565 / 1,051
NCSLGR (SignStream, 2007)	ASL-English	1,875	2,484 / 3,104
RWTH-PHOENIX-Weather 2014T (Camgoz et al., 2018)	DGS-German	7,096 + 519 + 642	1,066 / 2,887 + 393 / 951 + 411 / 1,001
Dicta-Sign-LSF-v2 (Limsi, 2019)	French SL-French	2,904	2,266 / 5,028
The Public DGS Corpus (Hanke et al., 2020)	DGS-German	63,912	4,694 / 23,404

Table 1: Some publicly available SL corpora with gloss annotations and spoken language translations.

3 Sign vs. Spoken Language

Due to the paucity of parallel data for gloss-to-text translation, we can treat it as a low-resource translation problem and apply existing techniques for improving accuracy in such settings.

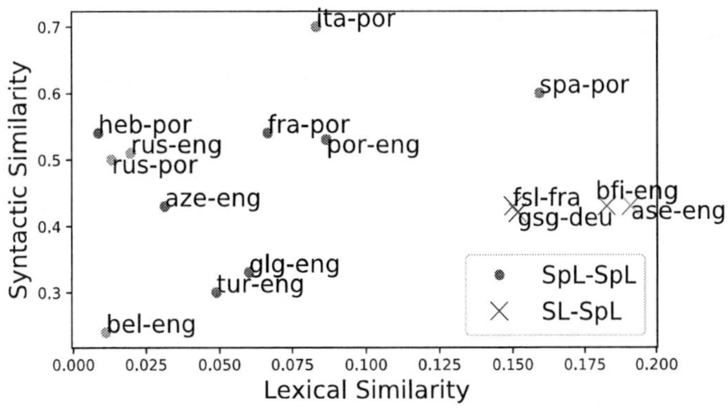

Figure 2: Lexical and syntactic similarity between different language pairs denoted by their ISO639-2 codes.

However, we argue that the relationship between glossed SLs and their spoken counterparts is different from the usual relationship between two spoken languages. Specifically, glossed SLs are *lexically similar but syntactically different* from their spoken counterparts. This contrasts heavily with the relationship among spoken language pairs where lexically similar languages tend also to be syntactically similar the great majority of the time.

To demonstrate this empirically, we adopt measures from (Lin et al., 2019) to measure the lexical and syntactic similarity between languages, two features also shown to be positively correlated with the effectiveness of performing cross-lingual transfer in MT.

Lexical similarity between two languages is measured using word overlap:

$$o_w = \frac{|T_1 \cap T_2|}{|T_1| + |T_2|}$$

where T_1 and T_2 are the sets of types in a corpus for each language. The word overlap between spoken language pairs is calculated using the TED talks dataset (Qi et al., 2018). The overlap between sign-spoken language pairs is calculated from the corresponding corpora in Table 1.

Syntactic similarity between two languages is measured by $1 - d_{syn}$ where d_{syn} is the syntactic distance from (Littell et al., 2017) calculated by taking the cosine distance between syntactic features adapted from the World Atlas of Language Structures (Dryer and Haspelmath, 2013).

Figure 2 shows that sign-spoken language pairs are indeed outliers with lower syntactic similarity and higher lexical similarity. We seek to leverage this fact and the high availability of monolingual spoken language data to compensate for the scarcity of SL resources. In the following section, we propose data augmentation techniques using word order modifications to create synthetic sign gloss data from spoken language corpora.

4 Data Augmentation

This section discusses methods to improve gloss-to-text translation through data augmentation, specifically those that take monolingual corpora of standard spoken languages and generate pseudo-parallel "gloss" text. We first discuss a standard way of doing so, back-translation, point out its potential failings in the SL setting, then propose a novel rule-based data augmentation algorithm.

4.1 Back-translation

Back-translation (Irvine and Callison-Burch, 2013; Sennrich et al., 2016a) automatically creates pseudo-parallel sentence pairs from monolingual text to improve MT in low-resource settings. However, back-translation is only effective with sufficient parallel data to train a functional MT model, which is not always the case in extremely low-resource settings (Currey et al., 2017), and particularly when the domain of the parallel training data and monolingual data to be translated are mismatched (Dou et al., 2020).

4.2 Proposed Rule-based Augmentation Strategies

Given the limitations of standard back-translation techniques, we next move to the proposed method of using rule-based heuristics to generate SL glosses from spoken language text.

General rules The differences in SL glosses from spoken language can be summarized by (1) A lack of word inflection, (2) An omission of punctuation and individual words, and (3) Syntactic diversity.

We, therefore, propose the corresponding three heuristics to generate pseudo-glosses from spoken language: (1) Lemmatization of spoken words; (2) POS-dependent and random word deletion; (3) Random word permutation.

We use spaCy (Honnibal and Montani, 2017) for (1) lemmatization and (2) POS tagging to only keep nouns, verbs, adjectives, adverbs, and numerals. We also drop the remaining tokens with probability $p = 0.2$, and (3) randomly reorder tokens with maximum distance $d = 4$.

Language-specific rules While random permutation allows some degree of robustness to word order, it cannot capture all aspects of syntactic divergence between signed and spoken language. Therefore, inspired by previous work on rule-based syntactic transformations for reordering in MT (Collins et al., 2005; Isozaki et al., 2010; Zhou et al., 2019), we manually devise a shortlist of syntax transformation rules based on the grammar of DGS and German.

We perform lemmatization and POS filtering as before. In addition, we apply compound splitting (Tuggener, 2016) on nouns and only keep the first noun, reorder German SVO sentences to SOV, move adverbs and location words to the start of the sentence, and move negation words to the end. We provide a detailed list of rules in Appendix A.

5 Experimental Setting

5.1 Datasets

DGS & German RWTH-PHOENIX-Weather 2014T (Camgoz et al., 2018) is a parallel corpus of 8,257 DGS interpreted videos from the Phoenix[1] weather news channel, with corresponding SL glosses and German translations.

To obtain monolingual German data, we crawled tagesschau[2] and extracted news caption files containing the word "wetter" (German for "weather"). We split the 1,506 caption files into 341,023 German sentences using the spaCy sentence splitter and generate synthetic glosses using our methods described in §4.

ASL & English The NCSLGR dataset (SignStream, 2007) is a small, general domain dataset containing 889 ASL videos with 1,875 SL glosses and English translations.

We use ASLG-PC12 (Othman and Jemni, 2012), a large synthetic ASL gloss dataset created from English text using rule-based methods with 87,710 publicly available examples, for our experiments on ASL-English with language-specific rules. We also create another synthetic variation of this dataset using our proposed general rule-based augmentation.

[1] www.phoenix.de

[2] www.tagesschau.de

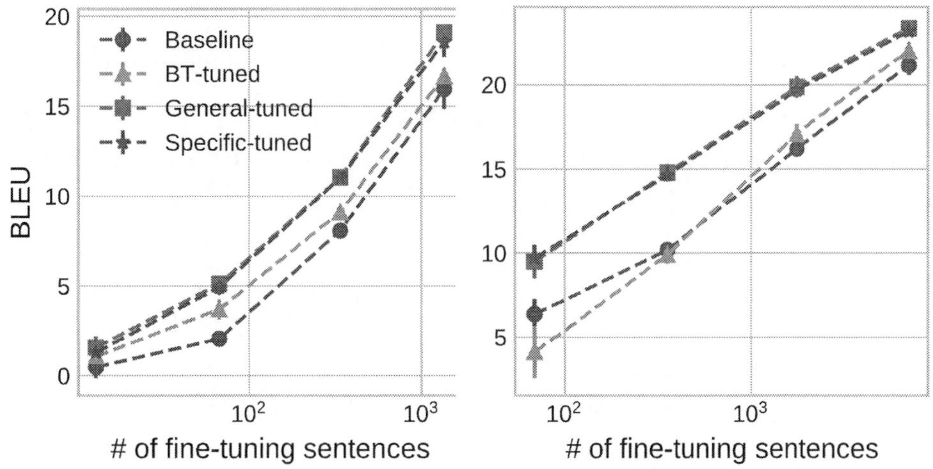

(a) NCSLGR (ASL) (b) PHOENIX (DGS)

Figure 3: Translation results using various amounts of annotated parallel data.

5.2 Baseline Setup

We first train a **Baseline** system on the small manually annotated SL dataset we have available in each language pair. The model architecture and training method are based on Yin and Read (2020b)'s Transformer gloss-to-text translation model. While previous work (**Yin and Read Reimpl.**) used word-level tokenization, for Baseline and all other models described below, we instead use BPE tokenization (Sennrich et al. (2016b); with 2,000 BPE codes) for efficiency and simple handling of unknown words. For all tested methods, we repeat every experiment 3 times to account for variance in training.

5.3 Pre-training on Augmented Data

For **General-*pre*** and **Specific-*pre***, we pre-train a tokenizer and translation model on pseudo-parallel data obtained using general and language-specific rules respectively, until the accuracy on the synthetic validation set drops. We test both models on the parallel SL dataset in a zero-shot setting.

For **BT-*tuned***, **General-*tuned*** and **Specific-*tuned***, we take models pre-trained on pseudo-parallel data obtained with either back-translation, general rules, or language-specific rules, and continue training with half of the training data taken from the synthetic pseudo-parallel data and the other half taken from the real SL data. Then, we fine-tune these models on the real SL data and evaluate them on the test set.

6 Results

We evaluate our models across all datasets and sizes using SacreBLEU (v1.4.14) (Post, 2018) and COMET (*wmt-large-da-estimator-1719*) (Rei et al., 2020). We also compare our results to previous work on PHOENIX in Table 2. Detailed scores for each experiment are provided in Appendix C.

First, we note results on General-*pre* and Specific-*pre*. Interestingly, the scores are non-

	PHOENIX		NCSLGR	
	BLEU↑	COMET↑	BLEU↑	COMET↑
Yin and Read Reimpl.[4]	22.17	-2.93	-	-
Baseline	21.15	-5.74	15.95	-61.00
General-*pre* (0-shot)	3.95	-69.09	0.97	-135.99
Specific-*pre* (0-shot)	7.26	-53.14	0.95	-134.13
BT-*tuned*	**22.02**	**6.84**	16.67	**-51.86**
General-*tuned*	**23.35**	**13.65**	**19.09**	**-34.50**
Specific-*tuned*	**23.17**	**11.70**	**18.58**	**-39.96**

Table 2: Results of our different models on PHOENIX and NCSLGR. We **bold** scores statistically significantly higher than baseline at the 95% confidence level.

negligible, demonstrating that the model can learn with *only* augmented data.[3] Moreover, on PHOENIX Specific-*pre* achieves significantly better performance than General-*pre*, which suggests our hand-crafted syntax transformations effectively expose the model to the divergence between DGS and German during pre-training.

Next, turning to the *tuned* models, we see that Specific and General outperform both the baseline and BT by large margins, demonstrating the effectiveness of our proposed methods. Interestingly, General-*tuned* performs slightly better, in contrast to the previous result. We posit that, similarly to previously reported results on sampling-based back translation (Edunov et al., 2018), General is benefiting from the diversity provided by sampling multiple reordering candidates, even if each candidate is of lower quality.

Looking at Figure 3, we see that the superior performance of our methods holds for all data sizes, but it is particularly pronounced when the parallel-data-only baseline achieves moderate BLEU scores in the range of 5-20. This confirms that BT is not a viable data augmentation method when parallel data is not plentiful enough to train a robust back-translation system.

7 Implications and Future Work

Consistent improvements over the baseline across two language pairs by our proposed rule-based augmentation strategies demonstrate that data augmentation using monolingual spoken language data is a promising approach for sign language translation.

Given the efficiency of our general rules compared to language-specific rules, future work may also include a more focused approach on specifically pre-training the target-side decoder with spoken language sentences so that by learning the syntax of the target spoken language, it can generate fluent sentences from sign language glosses having little to no parallel examples during training.

[3] In contrast, merely outputting the source sentence results in 1.36 BLEU, -90.28 COMET on PHOENIX and 1.5 BLEU, -119.45 COMET on NCSLGR.

[4] The original work achieves 23.32 BLEU; correspondence with the authors has led us to believe that the discrepancy is due to different versions of the underlying software.

References

Bragg, D., Koller, O., Bellard, M., Berke, L., Boudreault, P., Braffort, A., Caselli, N., Huenerfauth, M., Kacorri, H., Verhoef, T., et al. (2019). Sign language recognition, generation, and translation: An interdisciplinary perspective. In *The 21st International ACM SIGACCESS Conference on Computers and Accessibility*, pages 16–31.

Camgoz, N. C., Hadfield, S., Koller, O., Ney, H., and Bowden, R. (2018). Neural sign language translation. In *Proceedings of the IEEE Conference on Computer Vision and Pattern Recognition (CVPR)*.

Camgoz, N. C., Koller, O., Hadfield, S., and Bowden, R. (2020). Sign language transformers: Joint end-to-end sign language recognition and translation. In *IEEE Conference on Computer Vision and Pattern Recognition (CVPR)*.

Collins, M., Koehn, P., and Kučerová, I. (2005). Clause restructuring for statistical machine translation. In *Proceedings of the 43rd Annual Meeting of the Association for Computational Linguistics (ACL'05)*, pages 531–540, Ann Arbor, Michigan. Association for Computational Linguistics.

Cui, R., Liu, H., and Zhang, C. (2017). Recurrent convolutional neural networks for continuous sign language recognition by staged optimization. In *Proceedings of the IEEE Conference on Computer Vision and Pattern Recognition*, pages 7361–7369.

Currey, A., Miceli Barone, A. V., and Heafield, K. (2017). Copied monolingual data improves low-resource neural machine translation. In *Proceedings of the Second Conference on Machine Translation*, pages 148–156, Copenhagen, Denmark. Association for Computational Linguistics.

Dou, Z.-Y., Anastasopoulos, A., and Neubig, G. (2020). Dynamic data selection and weighting for iterative back-translation. In *Proceedings of the 2020 Conference on Empirical Methods in Natural Language Processing (EMNLP)*, pages 5894–5904, Online. Association for Computational Linguistics.

Dryer, M. S. and Haspelmath, M., editors (2013). *WALS Online*. Max Planck Institute for Evolutionary Anthropology, Leipzig.

Edunov, S., Ott, M., Auli, M., and Grangier, D. (2018). Understanding back-translation at scale. In *Proceedings of the 2018 Conference on Empirical Methods in Natural Language Processing*, pages 489–500, Brussels, Belgium. Association for Computational Linguistics.

Hanke, T., Schulder, M., Konrad, R., and Jahn, E. (2020). Extending the Public DGS Corpus in size and depth. In *Proceedings of the LREC2020 9th Workshop on the Representation and Processing of Sign Languages: Sign Language Resources in the Service of the Language Community, Technological Challenges and Application Perspectives*, pages 75–82, Marseille, France. European Language Resources Association (ELRA).

Honnibal, M. and Montani, I. (2017). spaCy 2: Natural language understanding with Bloom embeddings, convolutional neural networks and incremental parsing. To appear.

Irvine, A. and Callison-Burch, C. (2013). Combining bilingual and comparable corpora for low resource machine translation. In *Proceedings of the Eighth Workshop on Statistical Machine Translation*, pages 262–270, Sofia, Bulgaria. Association for Computational Linguistics.

Isozaki, H., Sudoh, K., Tsukada, H., and Duh, K. (2010). Head finalization: A simple reordering rule for sov languages. In *Proceedings of the Joint Fifth Workshop on Statistical Machine Translation and MetricsMATR*, pages 244–251.

Klein, G., Kim, Y., Deng, Y., Senellart, J., and Rush, A. (2017). OpenNMT: Open-source toolkit for neural machine translation. In *Proceedings of ACL 2017, System Demonstrations*, pages 67–72, Vancouver, Canada. Association for Computational Linguistics.

Limsi (2019). Dicta-sign-lsf-v2. ORTOLANG (Open Resources and TOols for LANGuage) –www.ortolang.fr.

Lin, Y.-H., Chen, C.-Y., Lee, J., Li, Z., Zhang, Y., Xia, M., Rijhwani, S., He, J., Zhang, Z., Ma, X., Anastasopoulos, A., Littell, P., and Neubig, G. (2019). Choosing transfer languages for cross-lingual learning. In *Proceedings of the 57th Annual Meeting of the Association for Computational Linguistics*, pages 3125–3135, Florence, Italy. Association for Computational Linguistics.

Littell, P., Mortensen, D. R., Lin, K., Kairis, K., Turner, C., and Levin, L. (2017). URIEL and lang2vec: Representing languages as typological, geographical, and phylogenetic vectors. In *Proceedings of the 15th Conference of the European Chapter of the Association for Computational Linguistics: Volume 2, Short Papers*, pages 8–14, Valencia, Spain. Association for Computational Linguistics.

Ormel, E., Crasborn, O., van der Kooij, E., van Dijken, L., Nauta, E., Forster, J., and Stein, D. (2010). Glossing a multi-purpose sign language corpus. In *Proceedings of the 4th Workshop on the Representation and Processing of Sign Languages: Corpora and sign language technologies*, pages 186–191.

Othman, A. and Jemni, M. (2012). English-asl gloss parallel corpus 2012: Aslg-pc12. In *5th Workshop on the Representation and Processing of Sign Languages: Interactions between Corpus and Lexicon LREC*.

Post, M. (2018). A call for clarity in reporting BLEU scores. In *Proceedings of the Third Conference on Machine Translation: Research Papers*, pages 186–191, Brussels, Belgium. Association for Computational Linguistics.

Qi, Y., Sachan, D., Felix, M., Padmanabhan, S., and Neubig, G. (2018). When and why are pre-trained word embeddings useful for neural machine translation? In *Proceedings of the 2018 Conference of the North American Chapter of the Association for Computational Linguistics: Human Language Technologies, Volume 2 (Short Papers)*, pages 529–535, New Orleans, Louisiana. Association for Computational Linguistics.

Rei, R., Stewart, C., Farinha, A. C., and Lavie, A. (2020). COMET: A neural framework for MT evaluation. In *Proceedings of the 2020 Conference on Empirical Methods in Natural Language Processing (EMNLP)*, pages 2685–2702, Online. Association for Computational Linguistics.

Sennrich, R., Haddow, B., and Birch, A. (2016a). Improving neural machine translation models with monolingual data. In *Proceedings of the 54th Annual Meeting of the Association for Computational Linguistics (Volume 1: Long Papers)*, pages 86–96, Berlin, Germany. Association for Computational Linguistics.

Sennrich, R., Haddow, B., and Birch, A. (2016b). Neural machine translation of rare words with subword units. In *Proceedings of the 54th Annual Meeting of the Association for Computational Linguistics (Volume 1: Long Papers)*, pages 1715–1725, Berlin, Germany. Association for Computational Linguistics.

SignStream, N. (2007). Volumes 2–7.

Tuggener, D. (2016). *Incremental coreference resolution for German*. PhD thesis, University of Zurich.

Vaswani, A., Shazeer, N., Parmar, N., Uszkoreit, J., Jones, L., Gomez, A. N., Kaiser, L. u., and Polosukhin, I. (2017). Attention is all you need. In Guyon, I., Luxburg, U. V., Bengio, S., Wallach, H., Fergus, R., Vishwanathan, S., and Garnett, R., editors, *Advances in Neural Information Processing Systems*, volume 30, pages 5998–6008. Curran Associates, Inc.

von Agris, U. and Kraiss, K. (2007). Towards a video corpus for signer-independent continuous sign language recognition. In *Gesture in Human-Computer Interaction and Simulation*.

Xia, M., Kong, X., Anastasopoulos, A., and Neubig, G. (2019). Generalized data augmentation for low-resource translation. In *Proceedings of the 57th Annual Meeting of the Association for Computational Linguistics*, pages 5786–5796, Florence, Italy. Association for Computational Linguistics.

Yin, K. and Read, J. (2020a). Attention is all you sign: Sign language translation with transformers. In *Sign Language Recognition, Translation and Production (SLRTP) Workshop - Extended Abstracts*.

Yin, K. and Read, J. (2020b). Better sign language translation with stmc-transformer. In *Proceedings of the 28th International Conference on Computational Linguistics*.

Zhou, C., Ma, X., Hu, J., and Neubig, G. (2019). Handling syntactic divergence in low-resource machine translation. In *Proceedings of the 2019 Conference on Empirical Methods in Natural Language Processing and the 9th International Joint Conference on Natural Language Processing (EMNLP-IJCNLP)*, pages 1388–1394, Hong Kong, China. Association for Computational Linguistics.

Zoph, B., Yuret, D., May, J., and Knight, K. (2016). Transfer learning for low-resource neural machine translation. In *Proceedings of the 2016 Conference on Empirical Methods in Natural Language Processing*, pages 1568–1575, Austin, Texas. Association for Computational Linguistics.

A Data Augmentation Rules

A.1 General Rules

For a given sentence $\mathcal{S}$:

1. Discard all tokens $t \in \mathcal{S}$ if **POS**$(t) \notin$ {noun, verb, adjective, adverb, numeral}
2. Discard remaining tokens $t \in \mathcal{S}$ with probability $p = 0.2$
3. Lemmatize all tokens $t \in \mathcal{S}$
4. Apply a random permutation σ to $\mathcal{S}$ verifying $\forall i \in \{1, n\}, |\sigma(i) - i| \leq 4$

where n is the number of tokens in $\mathcal{S}$ at step 4 and **POS** is a part-of-speech tagger.

A.2 German-DGS Rules

For a given sentence $\mathcal{S}$:

1. For each subject-verb-object triplet $(s, v, o) \in \mathcal{S}$, swap the positions of v and o in $\mathcal{S}$
2. Discard all tokens $t \in \mathcal{S}$ if **POS**$(t) \notin$ {noun, verb, adjective, adverb, numeral}
3. For $t \in \mathcal{S}$, if **POS**$(t) =$ adverb, then move t to the start of s
4. For $t \in \mathcal{S}$, if **NER**$(t) =$ location, then move t to the start of s
5. For $t \in \mathcal{S}$, if **DEP**$(t) =$ negation, then move t to the end of s
6. For $t \in \mathcal{S}$, if t is a compound noun $c_1c_2...c_n$, replace t by c_1
7. Lemmatize all tokens $t \in \mathcal{S}$

where **POS** is a part-of-speech tagger, **NER** is a named entity recognizer and **DEP** is a dependency parser.

B Model Reproduction

For reproduction purposes, here we lay the exact commands for training a single model using OpenNMT 1.2.0 (Klein et al., 2017). These commands are taken from (Yin and Read, 2020b).

Given 6 files—*train.gloss* / *train.txt*, *dev.gloss* / *dev.txt*, *test.gloss* / *test.txt*—we start by preprocessing the data using the following command:

```
onmt_preprocess -dynamic_dict -save_data processed_data \
-train_src train.gloss -train_tgt train.txt -valid_src dev.gloss -valid_tgt dev.txt
```

Then, we train a translation system using the train command:

```
onmt_train -data processed_data -save_model model -layers 2 -rnn_size 512 -word_vec_size 512 -heads 8 \
-encoder_type transformer -decoder_type transformer -position_encoding -transformer_ff 2048 -dropout 0.1 \
-early_stopping 3 -early_stopping_criteria accuracy ppl -batch_size 2048 -accum_count 3 -batch_type tokens \
-max_generator_batches 2 -normalization tokens -optim adam -adam_beta2 0.998 -decay_method noam \
-warmup_steps 3000 -learning_rate 0.5 -max_grad_norm 0 -param_init 0 -param_init_glorot -label_smoothing 0.1 \
-valid_steps 100 -save_checkpoint_steps 100 -world_size 1 -gpu_ranks 0
```

At the end of the training procedure, it prints to console "Best model found at step X". Locate it, and use it for translating the data:

```
onmt_translate -model model_step_X.pt -src test.gloss -output hyp.txt -gpu 0 -replace_unk -beam_size 4
```

Finally, evaluate the output using SacreBLEU:

```
cat hyp.txt | sacrebleu test.txt
```

C Full Experimental Results

Table 3 includes the evaluation scores for all of our experiments, ran three times.

% of available annotated data used		1%		5%		25%		100%	
		BLEU	COMET	BLEU	COMET	BLEU	COMET	BLEU	COMET
PHOENIX	Baseline	6.37 ± 0.89	-89.21 ± 12.82	10.18 ± 0.40	-71.37 ± 2.86	16.20 ± 0.27	-33.88 ± 4.35	21.15 ± 0.58	-5.74 ± 2.35
	BT-*tuned*	4.12 ± 1.55	-91.87 ± 16.35	9.91 ± 0.54	**-53.38 ± 4.04**	**17.10 ± 0.56**	**-16.46 ± 2.52**	**22.02 ± 0.50**	**6.84 ± 0.34**
	General-*tuned*	**9.49 ± 1.01**	**-52.23 ± 6.31**	**14.78 ± 0.51**	**-27.13 ± 2.29**	**19.86 ± 0.64**	**-0.72 ± 2.44**	**23.35 ± 0.22**	**13.65 ± 1.68**
	Specific-*tuned*	**9.70 ± 0.75**	**-55.94 ± 2.08**	**14.65 ± 0.29**	**-30.85 ± 1.45**	**19.66 ± 0.08**	**-5.62 ± 0.51**	**23.17 ± 0.30**	**11.70 ± 1.20**
NCSLGR	Baseline	0.47 ± 0.60	-153.90 ± 11.89	2.07 ± 0.32	-145.14 ± 1.15	8.07 ± 0.43	-101.24 ± 5.14	15.95 ± 1.11	-61.00 ± 6.86
	BT-*tuned*	1.07 ± 0.47	**-139.80 ± 3.78**	**3.71 ± 0.55**	**-117.33 ± 3.03**	**9.11 ± 0.05**	**-82.41 ± 2.29**	16.67 ± 0.32	**-51.86 ± 0.66**
	General-*tuned*	1.58 ± 0.60	**-134.22 ± 1.73**	**5.13 ± 0.15**	**-106.59 ± 1.56**	**11.04 ± 0.04**	**-66.35 ± 2.00**	**19.09 ± 0.20**	**-34.50 ± 1.19**
	Specific-*tuned*	1.30 ± 0.52	**-128.14 ± 1.58**	**4.94 ± 0.45**	**-107.60 ± 4.01**	**10.99 ± 0.12**	**-71.37 ± 1.01**	**18.58 ± 0.84**	**-39.96 ± 1.91**

Table 3: Mean and standard deviation of BLEU and COMET over different experimental settings. We **bold** scores statistically significantly higher than baseline at the 95% confidence level.

Is "good enough" good enough? Ethical and responsible development of sign language technologies[1]

Maartje De Meulder

Abstract

This paper identifies some common and specific pitfalls in the development of sign language technologies targeted at deaf communities, with a specific focus on signing avatars. It makes the call to urgently interrogate some of the ideologies behind those technologies, including issues of ethical and responsible development. The paper addresses four separate and interlinked issues: ideologies about deaf people and mediated communication, bias in data sets and learning, user feedback, and applications of the technologies. The paper ends with several take away points for both technology developers and deaf NGOs. Technology developers should give more consideration to diversifying their team and working interdisciplinary, and be mindful of the biases that inevitably creep into data sets. There should also be a consideration of the technologies' end users. Sign language interpreters are not the end users nor should they be seen as the benchmark for language use. Technology developers and deaf NGOs can engage in a dialogue about how to prioritize application domains and prioritize *within* application domains. Finally, deaf NGOs policy statements will need to take a longer view, and use avatars to think of a significantly better system compared to what sign language interpreting services can provide.

Introduction

In our everyday lives, we increasingly (and often unconsciously) rely on technologies where the languages we see, hear and produce are mediated in real-time by technology. Indeed, we are well into the human-machine era (Sayers et al., 2021). We talk to our devices using Amazon's Alexa and Apple's Siri, we read tweets in different languages through Twitter's automatic translation feature, deaf people use Google Live Transcribe, Ava, and other apps for real-time speech-to-text access. All these features were built on years and years of human work, and years and years of training of machines. We know and accept that some of these features are far from perfect yet, but we use them anyway. Because these AI applications feed on data and our frequent use, technology is advancing quickly and improving all the time. Machines learn.

The last three decades have seen sign languages, and deaf people, who use these languages, as target groups of language technologies, being included in these efforts in various ways. This includes developments in automated translation from text-to-sign (e.g. Stoll et al., 2020), speech-to-sign (e.g. Cox et al., 2002; Glauert et al., 2006), or sign-to-text (currently still very limited, e.g. Camgöz et al., 2020a, b). The technology is being developed in the form of many existing technologies, for example wearable solutions like smart gloves and intelligent bots with sign language avatars (virtual humans). This makes it increasingly likely that we will sign to and through technology.

[1] The writing of this paper has benefited from ongoing discussions on this theme as part of the EU COST Action network 'Language in the Human Machine Era' https://lithme.eu/

Some of the technological solutions under development are campaigned and marketed as trailblazing, advanced developments, using cutting edge technologies. Inventors can be big tech companies but just as well hearing undergraduates who don't know any sign language. A good example is the robot-arm developed by hearing undergrad students who claimed this would advance deaf children's inclusion in education and could help "millions of deaf people". The only thing the robot arm could actually do, was rudimentary fingerspelling (Drewett, 2018). The rationales for developing these technologies 'for' deaf people often stem from a saviour complex ("we, abled people, need to help disabled people communicate"), and from "techno-solutionism" (Fleet, 2021) which leads to technology being developed uniformed by the lived experience of disabled people. Even so, these inventors often get significant press attention or even gain awards and grants from panels that do not include any signers (Lipomi, 2017). Most of these solutions are also one-way, placing the burden on deaf people (e.g. to wear smart gloves) so that 'hearing' people can understand them (Kouznetsova, 2016; Lu, 2016; Woodcock, 2012, 2020). There are also detectable ideologies behind sign-to-text technologies about the normativity of the spoken modality - in a sense, that deaf people's ideas make 'more sense' if converted to spoken form (Hill, 2013). Also, ideologies supporting the technologies reveal a lot about how deaf people are viewed and communication is normatively mediated.

Funded research projects in this field often claim that these technologies can assist with 'inclusion' of deaf people, 'social equality' and, finally, address the problem of the 'insufficient availability' and 'prohibitive costs' of sign language interpreting services. Recently funded and on-going projects in the EU attract quite a lot of funding, with the European Commission spending several millions of euro per project. Despite these claims, a lot of the technology is still notably limited in its development and usability. Also and importantly, much of the work has started and is on-going with minimal input from deaf communities (Erard, 2017).

This paper is not about the current technical limitations of language technologies for sign languages. These technologies have a lot of catching up to do compared to technologies for spoken languages. This will happen, one way or another. Instead, this paper addresses a more urgent issue: the ethical and responsible development of these technologies, specifically sign language avatars. This issue is currently virtually not discussed in the academic and practice community. Most publications on machine translation for sign languages are either technical accounts of how machine translation can work or uncritical technical evaluations of user experience (e.g. Kacorri et al., 2017, but see Quandt et al. 2021 for an exception). There are virtually no critical insights into ethical, societal, and ideological rationales for and consequences of technologies. Indeed, that discussion usually lags behind scientific innovation - ethical debates about new technologies often come after the fact of their use. But at least for sign languages, the lag time is becoming very long now, and there is a critical need to address some urgent questions.

Who invents the technologies, and what is their motivation for developing them? How are data being collected to make machines learn? Who evaluates the outcomes, and how? Is there an actual demand from the communities? Who are the end users and who decides that? Who benefits from these technologies, and who is at risk of being left behind? What are the current and potential future applications of those technologies? How will language rights keep pace with the development of language technologies? What are the ideologies behind these technologies?

This paper will mostly write from a Deaf Studies and sociolinguistics perspective, with a specific focus on sign language avatars (meaning communication towards sign language users). While I will semantically differentiate between the 'avatar' as the digital figure representing a (signing) person and the underlying 'translation engine' from or towards sign languages, for reasons of simplicity I will occasionally use the term 'avatar' to include the underlying translation engine. These avatars can be created in different ways. The movement can be based on recorded motion capture from real human signers or can be based on computer-synthesized motions. More recent innovations use machine learning trained on existing video data to generate these avatars. Those are the innovations this paper will mainly focus on, discussing research projects that have recently ended or are on-going in the European Union and the UK, such as Content4All[2], EASIER[3], SignON[4], SignLab at University of Amsterdam (UvA)[5], and aID – Artificial Intelligence for the Deaf[6]). It will address four separate and interlinked issues: ideologies about deaf people and mediated communication, bias in data sets and learning, user feedback, and applications of the technology. The paper ends with a few take away points for both technology developers and deaf NGOs.

Ideologies about deaf people/mediated communication

Several of the above-mentioned projects start from specific ideologies about deaf people and mediated communication: the researchers perceive a problematic 'communication gap' or 'language barrier' between 'deaf' and 'hearing' people, and state that technologies can and should address this gap or barrier. The main aim of the SignON project, prominent on the home page and the funder page, is to "bridge the communication gap between Deaf, hard of hearing and hearing people". It will "cross the language barrier between Deaf sign language users, hard of hearing and hearing people. SignON will tear down this information barrier that currently exists." The EASIER project is "bridging the communication gap between the deaf and the hearing". The aiD project offers "AI solutions for communicating needs of deaf people". The SignLab at UvA highlights "breaking language barriers". Stoll et al. (2018, p. 891) see the facilitation of "easy and clear communication between the hearing and the Deaf" as the critical aim of text-to-sign technologies, stating "... there is no guarantee that someone whose first language is, for example, British Sign Language, is familiar with written English, as the two are completely separate languages" (p. 892).

Some projects then make the leap to stating that their research can mitigate the problem of the limited availability and prohibitive costs of sign language interpreting services. SignON sees sign language interpreters as "the main medium for signed-to-spoken, spoken-to-signed and signed-to-signed translation", and the availability and costs of these services are seen as "a limiting factor in communication between signers and non-signers".

Some of the projects and the literature explicitly state the aim of language technologies for sign languages is not to *substitute* human interpreters but aim to be there for when interpreters are not available. The Content4All project proclaims that "systems that can accurately translate and produce sign would be of use to the Deaf. Not to replace human interpreters, but to provide translation into native sign language when an interpreter is not available (Young, 2020). A Dutch newspaper reporting on the development of sign language avatars at UvA headlined their piece "Sign language interpreters are scarce. Therefore an Amsterdam

---

[2] September 2017-November 2020, H2020 funding €4.1 million, https://content4all-project.eu/ and https://cordis.europa.eu/project/id/762021

[3] January 2021-December 2023, H2020 funding €3.9 million, https://www.project-easier.eu/vision/ and https://cordis.europa.eu/project/id/101016982

[4] January 2021-December 2023, H2020 funding €5.6 million, https://signon-project.eu/ and https://cordis.europa.eu/project/id/101017255

[5] https://www.signlab-amsterdam.nl/index.html NWO VICI grant or a 5-year project, funding €1.5 million.

[6] December 2019-November 2023, H2020 funding €1.5 million, https://aideaf.eu/ and https://cordis.europa.eu/project/id/872139

institute is learning an avatar to sign" and reported the lead researcher saying that "a human interpreter is always to be preferred above an avatar, when such an interpreter is available" (Zijlmans, 2021). Sáfár and Glauert state that "... in the deaf community, there is often a fear that the hard won recognition of their sign language will result in moves to make machines take over the role of human interpreters" (Sáfár & Glauert, 2012). The World Federation of the Deaf and World Association of Sign Language Interpreters (2018) statement on the use of signing avatars is the only one that uses different words to describe the risks and challenges: "the difference in linguistic quality between humans and avatars is why WFD and WASLI caution against the use of signing avatars as a replacement for human signers (World Federation of the Deaf & World Association of Sign Language Interpreters, 2018). The availability issue stands against experiences of deaf people being offered video remote interpreting (VRI) instead of sign language interpreters on location in some contexts, and their objections to this (e.g. Collinson, 2018). So, in reality, the 'unavailability' argument is a red herring – live interpreters *will* be substituted for avatars.

Another, related, aspect, is that the benchmark used to evaluate the quality of sign language technologies are often, again, sign language interpreters. Sayers et al. (2021, p. 10) assert that "consensus among the Deaf community so far is that these [smart gloves, avatars] are a profoundly poor substitute for human interpreters". Content4All affirms that "generating translations of the same quality as a human interpreter is extremely challenging". Sign language interpreters, not deaf signers themselves, are thus seen as language models, and as the benchmark for accepted standards of language use. If anything, this shows low ambition and an inability to see who the technology is for. Sign language interpreters are not the end users, nor should they be the benchmark.

With spoken languages there is the recognition that machine translation is at the moment of inferior quality compared to human *translators*, but that aspect is much less foregrounded and emphasized compared to the sign language projects. This is because the situation is profoundly different for deaf people, who are made reliant (by policy, legislation, and normative views on the role of sign language interpreting services) on sign language interpreters in many aspects of their lives. For deaf people, language rights often are paramount to access to sign language interpreters *in the first place* (De Meulder, 2016). But sign language interpreting services are, in many cases, a Band-Aid solution. They are not scalable services, and not equally available to deaf people who use them. They mostly benefit those deaf people with certain interpreter-related privileges. Even so, the provision of sign language interpreting services has become the institutionally normative, often unquestioned, solution to grant deaf people access to education and public services (De Meulder & Haualand, 2021).

Data sets and bias

In the context of machine learning, and more specifically the subtopic of Natural Language Processing (NLP) most sign languages tend to belong to the category of 'low-resourced languages'. The 'low-resourced' aspect refers to a lack of available training data and the fragmentation of efforts in resource development (Sayers et al., 2021). Indeed, NLP applications require large datasets to be available on which to train new algorithms. As NLP falls into the category of 'supervised learning', the algorithms learn by example in the form of 'labels', which tell the algorithm what needs to be learned. To allow this, large datasets must be labelled — which is expensive, time consuming, and prone to error, which can introduce bias. If the dataset is not carefully curated, it is mainly through these labels that bias can sneak into the algorithm. For sign languages there is the additional issue of a different language modality, which makes data collection and machine training much more challenging than it is between most spoken languages. Also, input in the form of text annotations in itself skews data sets because sign languages do not have a widely used written form (Jantunen et al., 2021).

Linked to this, there is the problem of generating data in a context of data sparsity and the risks for bias of language models. This is a common issue for NLP tools (Bender, 2019, 2021; Benjamin, 2020; Beukeboom and Burgers, 2017; Blodgett et al., 2020; Benjamin, 2020; Saleiro et al., 2020;). Dictionaries/lexicons for sign languages are developed for human use, not machine use (i.e. use by automated NLP systems). Digital sign language corpora have mostly focused on linguistic aspects (how signing is used) rather than computational processing (data from tracking movements, facial expressions, timing, etc.) (Sáfár & Glauert, 2012). These corpora are confronted with other problems that make them far less suitable for machine use linked to size and representativeness, and variety of discourses (Jantunen et al., 2021; Schembri & Cormier, 2022). In the absence of (semi-) automated annotation, manual annotation is demanding and time-consuming. This means that while for some sign languages there *is* a set of videorecorded data (although still small compared to most data sets for spoken languages), these are not suitable for machine learning because they are not, or only partially, annotated. Even if there is annotation, some of the larger sign language corpora currently only have basic annotation such as glosses and possibly translations but no other tags that can be provided by semi-automatic tagging tools (Hochesang, 2021; Schembri & Cormier, 2022).

On the other hand, we have to resign to, and therefore deal with, the realisation that machines are and will be trained on those corpora, which in themselves by design contain all the biases of the humans who design and assemble them (Saleiro et al., 2020). The largest sign language corpora now have participants numbering in the hundreds, but are often skewed by a native speaker bias, preferring focus on (often white) deaf native signers or early learners, who often went to residential schools (e.g. Schembri et al., 2013, for BSL). Jantunen et al. (2021, p. 4-5) go so far as to say that "the contribution of novices and non-native signers means decreased quality and accuracy" in corpora, and "to increase validity and recognition systems should be trained with real (native or near native) signers in realistic scenarios". At the same time, they state that "datasets should include representative, generalizable samples from diverse age groups, gender, culture, various ethnicities, varying body types and physical traits, clothes, lighting conditions and more". Work has been done on the development of more specialised corpora (see Schembri & Cormier, 2022). These focus on e.g. L2 learners (Mesch & Schönström, 2018), but not (yet) on, for example, signers from different racial and educational backgrounds, signers with immigration backgrounds, language deprivation, various disabilities, etc.

Due to this context of data scarcity, some of the on-going EU-funded projects start to collect their own data sets to train machines, using readily available internet data. In some cases, these are interpreted datasets. In these datasets both the signed input from the interpreter and the spoken source languages are available (or in the opposite case, the signed source language and the spoken output from the interpreter). This is also made possible by the COVID-19 pandemic, which led to an increase in recorded interpreted presentations, classes, press conferences etc. which are often available online. These datasets (with both deaf and hearing interpreters) are used as a training phase for machines to quickly enlarge the dataset.

In this stage already there is a significant risk for how bias can creep into the system when machines are trained on amalgams of data sets with input produced by either primarily white, native signers, or by interpreters. This is even more cause for concern combined with two related issues. The first is that sign language interpreters are often *already* language models for deaf learners in regular education (Caselli et al., 2020) and deaf people *already* often need to adapt their signing to be understood by interpreters. The second is that there is a realistic future possibility that signing avatars are going to be used to train sign language interpreting students. This would happen in an already problematic context of sign language interpreting training programs in general not reflecting racial diversity and multicultural, multilingual deaf community needs (Robinson et al., 2020).

User feedback

Thirdly, there is the issue of user feedback. When prototypes of avatars are developed, the developers need feedback from end users. In two cases (SignLab UvA and Content4All) this is/was done by an online survey in which (self-selected) deaf people are given specific tasks based on a pre-determined set of responses.

In the SignLab project deaf people are asked how well they understand translations by an animated avatar (using SiGML for sign language synthesis) compared to video translation by a deaf signer, specifically in a medical setting. Similarly, in the Content4All survey respondents look at an animated avatar and a deaf signer translating the weather forecast and are given specific tasks to evaluate comprehension. For example, they have to indicate which Dutch words they understood from the signing, given multiple options, answer questions (e.g., where do the clouds go to, what did the moderator suggest doing tomorrow?) and then indicate how sure they are of their response. At the start of the survey, it is specifically asked to give opinions "on comprehension of the signs rather than the look of the avatar" – as if the two can be separated.

Although asking user feedback is important, there are also several issues that must be addressed, and it is here where interdisciplinary approaches and specifically input from Deaf Studies researchers is most critically needed. Most deaf people have a life-long experience understanding different signing styles, of widely varying quality (see also Green, 2014 and Kusters et al., 2020 work on 'understanding'). The risk with asking this kind of user feedback is that deaf people will see avatars' signing as another signing style they'll have to put up with and learn to 'understand' (just as they need to learn to understand interpreters' signing). This can lead to socially desirable responses. This is related to what Woodcock (2020) in this context calls a "mouse on the doormat design" and the savior complex of some inventors: respondents might say they understood just because they think they are expected to appreciate this technology that is made 'for' them. A third issue is the uncanny valley (Mori et al., 2012) which might make viewers uncomfortable when confronted with simulations that closely resemble humans but are not quite convincing enough. We regard a Toy Story character which is obviously not human, as cute, but an avatar which is meant to be human but is not, as creepy. This combined with most deaf respondents not having realistic (or just not having any) expectations about avatars (see also Sáfár & Glauert, 2012). While some deaf people are trained to manage expectations about sign language interpreters (knowing the limitations of interpretation) and may tolerate the limitations of Google Translate or existing speech-to-text technologies, most deaf people are not yet used to manage expectations about the robotic and unarticulated signing of most avatars. This means that either expectations can be too low so that ratings will be higher than reasonably justified, or that on the contrary expectations are too high. Add to this the lack of testing in real-world settings. Indeed, there is a big difference from watching an avatar from a screen in your own office for a short experiment, and having to watch it during a nerve-wrecking medical appointment. This is not just unintentionally creepy entertainment in the uncanny valley, when you can look away (Woodcock, 2020). If your health depends on it, you cannot afford to look away. Evaluations do not account for this.

Applications

A last issue are current and future applications of language technologies for sign languages, such as avatars. The use of those technologies in the context of highly constrained and predictable domains such as tourism or travelling could be reasonably justified. An avatar might be used to make an order in a coffee house, check in in a hotel, have access to announcements at airports or railway stations, or for interaction with specific customer services. Another potentially useful application of avatars could be in those situations where sensitive, confidential information must be shared (by a deaf person themselves or a human interpreter) and where this person prefers to remain anonymous, and in areas where deaf people feel uncomfortable about the presence of interpreters (see also Quandt et al. 2021).

However, some starter projects beginning with very fundamental limitations as outlined above, at this point already go directly into sensitive areas such as the medical domain (e.g. Roelofsen et al., 2021[7]). This happens despite explicit statements and warnings by authoritative deaf NGOs such as the WFD and WASLI that the medical domain is a no-go area. These NGOs expressed concerns on the use of avatars "when the information being delivered is live, complex or of significant importance to the lives of deaf citizens" (World Federation of the Deaf & World Association of Sign Language Interpreters, 2018). Applications in the medical domain have been spurred by the COVID-19 pandemic, which exposed communication problems between health care professionals and deaf people when everyone had to wear facemasks, interpreters were often not allowed in hospitals and interpreting via video relay was not always viable.

That this is happening in the first place, is again linked to how deaf people are viewed, and how communication is currently normatively mediated by sign language interpreters. Sign language interpreters, on location or remotely, are accepted for mediated healthcare communication, despite critical limitations (Kushalnagar et al., 2019). Because this practice is largely accepted and even normative, use of language technologies in healthcare situations is seen as the logical next step and as a justified application domain by technology developers.

Conclusion

This paper has identified some common and specific pitfalls in the development of sign language technologies targeted at deaf communities and has made the call to urgently interrogate the ideologies behind those technologies, including issues of ethical and responsible development. What has been done technologically so far is very promising, but if continued on the same path, there is a risk that technologies developed in the end will not be voluntarily adopted by end users. This uptake in use is important, because the more 'we' use AI, the better it will become. There must be a consideration though of who this 'we' is – who is the language technology for, and why? Sign language interpreters are not the end users here, nor should they be seen as the benchmark for language use. Placing interpreters on the centre of deaf peoples' lives (a constructed dependence) comes from a biased and hearing-centred view on communication.

For the technology developers, this paper makes the call to *diversify the team* and *work interdisciplinary.* Co-design or co-engineer (see also Jantunen et al., 2021) with the end users

[7] For demo see here https://www.signlab-amsterdam.nl/healthcare-demo.html

of the language technologies, a widely varied group of deaf people. Not just to ensure semantic value, but also to ensure that technologies are being developed incorporating the communities demands, values, and feedback, that there is given consideration to interaction design and user interfaces. Engage in interdisciplinary collaborations, combining Deaf Studies, language policy, sign linguistics, Sign Language Interpreting Studies, computer science, sociolinguistics, Human Computer Interaction, artificial intelligence, computational linguistics, etc., not only in the execution of research projects but also in writing and reviewing them.

Regarding data sets, this paper is not meant as a discouragement for researchers from advancing the state of the art. If there is a need to wait for the 'perfect' datasets to appear (which might never happen) instead of using what is readily available, the delay for practical working solutions might become much longer. This is a call though to at the very minimum *be mindful of the biases* that will inevitably creep into data sets, and to consider the long-term implications of this.

Regarding applications, there are some take-away points both for developers of technologies and for deaf NGOs who need to evaluate their use and application domains. At this point, many projects are using signing avatars to do many different things, in many different ways – some of which are probably less problematic, and some of which are more. A deaf tech developer and artist working on incorporating signed language into VR spaces is a very different development and application compared to a hearing non-signing engineer developing a signing avatar without any consultation or collaboration with deaf communities. For the developers of technologies and for deaf NGOs there are two takeaway points:
(1) *Prioritize the application domains*: there is a significant distinction to be made between for example an avatar presenting information on a government webpage, or an avatar used to mediate communication during a life-threatening healthcare situation. There is a lot of unproblematic low-hanging fruit: it is thus important to identify those research agendas which are problematic, while leaving space for those who are not. This is even more a case for deaf academics to (co-)lead these projects and to involve deaf people in various roles, in various stages of review of project applications, project development, project execution, and evaluation. This will make it possible to identify early which research agendas *are* problematic, and how this can be potentially mitigated, and which research agendas are worth pursuing. This will advance the state of the art in such a way that it is more likely technologies will be adopted by end users.
(2) *Prioritize within application domains*: building on the previous point, it will be critical to make much finer distinctions per different uses per domain. For example it is not helpful to tar all applications in the medical domain with the same brush. Some might be useful and necessary, while others might remain a no-go.

For the deaf NGOs there are two further points to keep in mind.
(a) *Look at the horizon*: statements by for example WFD and WASLI are based on the *current* state of the art, which appropriately advises against the use of avatars "when the information being delivered is live, complex or of significant importance to the lives of deaf citizens" (World Federation of the Deaf & World Association of Sign Language Interpreters, 2018). The technologies developed so far just do not warrant use of avatars in those situations. But this is not a status quo, and technology is advancing all the time. Policy statements will need to take a much longer view. Here again, the questions from the introduction of this article come to the foreground. What are potential *future* applications of those technologies? Not based on the technologies as they are now, but based on how they will inevitably develop? How will language rights keep pace with the development of language technologies? Who benefits from these technologies, and who is at risk of being left behind?

(b) *Use avatars to think of a significantly better system*: much of the current ideological framework by which the use of avatars is assessed is based on experiences with sign language interpreting services. Deaf NGOs appropriately advise against use of avatars in situations where it is not warranted, but at the same time, sign language interpreting services are often used in situations where they are not warranted either. The political institution of sign language interpreting services leaves a lot of questions to be considered regarding scalability and fairness. Let's not substitute one imperfect system with another. Let's use this moment in time, these technological possibilities, to try and design a better system.

Acknowledgments

Thanks to Jan Adriaenssens, Lorna Quandt, Joseph Murray, Tanguy Coenen, Kristin Snoddon, and the two anonymous reviewers for their generous feedback on previous drafts of this paper.

References

Bender, E. (2019). A Typology of Ethical Risks in Language: Technology with an Eye Towards Where Transparent Documentation Can Help. https://faculty.washington.edu/ebender/papers/Bender-A-Typology.pdf

Benjamin, R. (2020). 2020 Vision: Reimagining the Default Settings of Technology & Society. https://iclr.cc/virtual_2020/speaker_3.html

Beukeboom, C. J., & Burgers, C. (2017). Linguistic bias. In H. Giles & J. Harwood (Eds.), *Oxford Encyclopedia of Intergroup Communication*. Oxford University Press.

Blodgett, S. L., Barocas, S., Daumé, H., & Wallach, H. (2020). *Language (technology) is power: A critical survey of bias.* In *Proceedings of the 58th Annual Meeting of the Association for Computational Linguistics* (pp. 454-476).

Camgöz, N.C., Koller, O., Hadfield, S., Bowden, R. (2020a). Multi-Channel Transformers for Multi-Articulatory Sign Language Translation. In *European Conference on Computer Vision,* 301-19.

Camgöz, N.C., Koller, O., Hadfield, S., Bowden, R. (2020b). Sign Language Transformers: Joint End-to-End Sign Language Recognition and Translation. In *Proceedings of the Ieee/Cvf Conference on Computer Vision and Pattern Recognition,* 10023-33.

Caselli, N. K., Hall, W. C., & Henner, J. (2020). American Sign Language Interpreters in Public Schools: An Illusion of Inclusion that Perpetuates Language Deprivation. *Maternal and Child Health Journal, 24*, 1323-1329.

Collinson, A. (2018). The deaf patients 'left behind' by the NHS. https://www.bbc.com/news/health-44384503

Cox, S., Lincoln, M., Tryggvason, J., Nakisa, M., Wells, M., Tutt, M., & Abbott, S. (2002). *TESSA, a system to aid communication with deaf people.* In *Proceedings of the 5th international ACM conference on assistive technologies* (pp. 205-212).

De Meulder, M. (2016). *The Power of Language Policy* [PhD]. University of Jyväskylä.

De Meulder, M., & Haualand, H. (2021). Sign language interpreting services: A quick fix for inclusion? *Translation and Interpreting Studies, 16*(1), 19-40. https://doi.org/10.1075/tis.18008.dem

Erard, M. (2017). *Why sign-language gloves don't help deaf people.* Retrieved 2019-05-16 from https://www.theatlantic.com/technology/archive/2017/11/why-sign-language-gloves-dont-help-deaf-people/545441/

Fleet, C. [@ChanceyFleet] (2021, June 27). *What's true of other marginalized groups is true of us: techno-solutionism, uninformed by our wisdom and lived experience, can only harm us and waste investors' dollars and reputations. Stop it.*[Tweet] https://twitter.com/ChanceyFleet/status/1409221969166352393

Glauert, J. R. W., Elliott, R., Cox, S. J., Tryggvason, J., & Sheard, M. (2006). VANESSA – A System for Communication between Deaf and Hearing People. *Technology and Disability*, *18*, 207-216.

Green, E. M. (2014). Building the tower of Babel: International Sign, linguistic commensuration, and moral orientation. *Language in Society*, *43*(4), 445-465.

Hill, J. (2013). Language ideologies, policies, and attitudes towards signed languages. In R. Bayley, R. Cameron, & C. Lucas (Eds.), *The Oxford Handbook of Sociolinguistics* (pp. 680-697). Oxford University Press.

Hochesang, J. (2021). Documenting Language Use of the ASL Communities. https://www.youtube.com/watch?v=CJtfRQ0tsfM

Jantunen, T., Rousi, R., Rainò, P., Turunen, M., Valipoor, M. M., & García, N. (2021). Is There Any Hope for Developing Automated Translation Technology for Sign Languages? In M. Hämäläinen, N. Partanen, & K. Alnajjar (Eds.), *Multilingual Falicitation* (pp. 1-13). University of Helsinki.

Kacorri, H., Huenerfauth, M., Ebling, S., Patel, K., Menzies, K., & Willard, M. (2017). Regression Analysis of Demographic and Technology-Experience Factors Influencing Acceptance of Sign Language Animation. *ACM Transactions on Accessible Computing (TACCESS)*, *10*(1), 3-33. https://doi.org/10.1145/3046787

Kouznetsova, S. (2016). Why the Signing Gloves Hype Needs to Stop - Audio Accessibility. https://audio-accessibility.com/news/2016/05/signing-gloves-hype-needs-stop/

Kushalnagar, P., Paludneviciene, R., & Kushalnagar, R. (2019). Video Remote Interpreting Technology in Health Care: Cross-Sectional Study of Deaf Patients' Experiences. *JMIR Rehabil Assist Technol*, *6*(1), 1-8.

Kusters, A., Green, M., Moriarty Harrelson, E., & Snoddon, K. (2020). Sign language ideologies: Practices and politics. In A. Kusters, M. Green, E. Moriarty Harrelson, & K. Snoddon (Eds.), *Sign Language Ideologies in Practice*. De Gruyter Mouton.

Lipomi, D. (2017). *Lessons from working with the press: Cultural considerations and terminology surrounding American Sign Language in engineering research.* Retrieved 2019-05-16 from https://www.lipomigroup.org/blog/2017/9/12/cultural-considerations-and-terminology-surrounding-american-sign-language-in-materials-research

Lu, A. (2016). Deaf People Don't Need New Communication Tools — Everyone Else Does. *httpsmedium.com.* https://medium.com/@alexijie/deaf-people-dont-need-new-communication-tools-everyone-else-does-df83b5eb28e7

Mitchell, R. E., & Karchmer, M. A. (2004). Chasing the mythical ten percent: Parental hearing status of deaf and hard of hearing students in the United States. *Sign Language Studies*, *4*(2), 138-163.

Mori, M., MacDorman, K. F., & Kageki, N. (2012). The Uncanny Valley [from the field]. *IEEE Robotics & Automation Magazine*, *19*, 98-100.

Robinson, O. E., Sheneman, N., & Henner, J. (2020). Toxic Ableism Among Interpreters: Impeding deaf people's linguistic rights through pathological posturing. In C. McDermid, S. Ehrlich, & A. Gentry (Eds.), *Conference proceedings of the 2019 WASLI conference* (pp. 14-41). WASLI.

Roelofsen, F., Mende-Gillings, S. E., Esselink, L. D., & Smeijers, A. S. (2021). Supporting dialogue between healthcare professionals and Deaf patients through automated text-to-sign translation. *https://www.signlab-amsterdam.nl/publications/COVID-19.pdf.*

Sáfár, E., & Glauert, J. (2012). Computer modelling. In R. Pfau, M. Steinbach, & B. Woll (Eds.), *Sign Language. An International Handbook* (pp. 1075-1101). De Gruyter Mouton.

Saleiro, P., Rodolfa, K. T., & Ghani, R. (2020). *Dealing with Bias and Fairness in Data Science Systems: A Practical Hands-On Tutorial.* In *Proceedings of the 26th ACM SIGKDD International Conference on Knowledge Discovery and Data Mining* (pp. 3513-3514).

Sayers, D., Sousa-Silva, S., & Höhn. (2021). The Dawn of the Human-Machine Era: A forecast of new and emerging language technologies. *Report for EU COST Action CA19102 'Language in the Human-Machine Era'.* https://doi.org/10.17011/jyx/reports/20210518/1

Schembri, A., & Cormier, K. (2022). Sign language corpora: future directions. In J. Hochesang & J. Fenlon (Eds.), *Sign language corpora.* Gallaudet University Press.

Stoll, S., Camgoz, N. C., Hadfield, S., & Bowden, R. (2020). Text2Sign: Towards Sign Language Production Using Neural Machine Translation and Generative Adversarial Networks. *International Journal of Computer Vision, 128*, 891-908. https://doi.org/https://doi.org/10.1007/s11263-019-01281-2

Woodcock, K. (2012). Pick up a pencil. https://safeandsilent.wordpress.com/2012/07/11/pencil/

Woodcock, K. (2020). Paved with good intentions. https://safeandsilent.wordpress.com/category/technology/

World Federation of the Deaf & World Association of Sign Language Interpreters. (2018). WFD and WASLI Issue Statement on Signing Avatars - WFD. https://wfdeaf.org/news/wfd-wasli-issue-statement-signing-avatars/

Young, G. (2020). Automated Sign Language to produce signs helping the Deaf, not the hearing…. https://content4all-project.eu/automated-sign-language-to-produce-signs-helping-the-deaf-not-the-hearing/

Zijlmans, M. (2021). – *De Volkskrant.* Retrieved 2021-06-17 from https://www.volkskrant.nl/wetenschap/gebarentolken-zijn-schaars-daarom-leert-een-amsterdams-instituut-een-avatar-gebarentaal~b4449e2b/

Sign and Search: Sign Search Functionality for Sign Language Lexica

Manolis Fragkiadakis m.fragkiadakis@hum.leidenuniv.nl
Leiden University Centre for Digital Humanities, Leiden University, Leiden, 2311VJ, the Netherlands

Peter van der Putten p.w.h.van.der.putten@liacs.leidenuniv.nl
Leiden Institute of Advanced Computer Sciences, Leiden University, Leiden, 2333CA, the Netherlands

Abstract

Sign language lexica are a useful resource for researchers and people learning sign languages. Current implementations allow a user to search a sign either by its gloss or by selecting its primary features such as handshape and location. This study focuses on exploring a reverse search functionality where a user can sign a query sign in front of a webcam and retrieve a set of matching signs. By extracting different body joints combinations (upper body, dominant hand's arm and wrist) using the pose estimation framework OpenPose, we compare four techniques (PCA, UMAP, DTW and Euclidean distance) as distance metrics between 20 query signs, each performed by eight participants on a 1200 sign lexicon. The results show that UMAP and DTW can predict a matching sign with an 80% and 71% accuracy respectively at the top-20 retrieved signs using the movement of the dominant hand arm. Using DTW and adding more sign instances from other participants in the lexicon, the accuracy can be raised to 90% at the top-10 ranking. Our results suggest that our methodology can be used with no training in any sign language lexicon regardless of its size.

1 Introduction

Sign language lexica are a valuable source for people learning sign languages, teachers and parents who need to communicate in signs with their deaf children as well as researchers studying the languages in question. These lexica allow the user to submit a query containing a unique identifier that by definition refers to a sign (commonly referred to as gloss) and retrieve a video or an image of that sign. In addition to this functionality, some lexica let the user define the formal parameters of the target sign (i.e. its location, handshape, or movement) and retrieve all the signs that contain these features. It is then at the users' discretion to view all the provided signs and select the desired ones. These search functionalities are particularly useful as sign languages, contrary to spoken languages, do not have any unified notation system for sign representation.

Even though a sign search functionality which is based on formal parameters is a user-friendly option in sign language lexica, it still requires manual annotation. Dictionary compilers have to manually link these values to the individual videos of signs. This is a time consuming and prone to errors task and, as Zwitserlood (2010) discusses, it is the reason why only a few of such dictionaries exist to date. More importantly, according to Zwitserlood, these dictionaries are unidirectional "giving only signed translations of words from a spoken language in a one-to-one relation" (Zwitserlood, 2010). Furthermore, as the retrieved results contain only the parameters selected by the user, the signs are presented in no particular order.

In this paper, we describe a methodology and its experimental results for multi-directional search functionality for sign language lexica. Our proposed method, extending on previous efforts by Schneider et al. (2019) and Fragkiadakis et al. (2020), utilizes either the Uniform Manifold Approximation and Projection for Dimension Reduction (UMAP) technique or the Dynamic Time Warping (DTW) algorithm to measure the distance between a query sign and all the signs in a lexicon. Both techniques require no training, thus making our methodology applicable to any sign language. Requiring training would add further obstacles to making dictionaries widely available, similar to how the need for manual annotation is limiting dictionary availability. Finally, these methods have been compared to two other techniques namely Principal Component Analysis (PCA) and Euclidean distance.

The paper is organized as follows: in Section 2 we discuss the research which has been conducted in relation to search functionality for sign language lexica or has the potential to be applied in that domain. In Section 3 we describe our methodology regarding the extraction of the body joint coordinates as well as the methods and algorithms compared in this study. In Section 4 we present the results of our experiments. We discuss them in Section 5 and conclude and motivate future research in Section 6.

2 Related Work

Over the last decade, many research projects have examined the use of computer-vision techniques to allow a user to search a sign in a database or lexicon by performing it in front of a camera or sensor. Wang et al. (2012) have developed a system for semi-automatic search functionality. In their system, a user marks the start and end frames of a sign and denotes whether the sign is one- or two-handed. Consequently, the system detects the hands on the basis of skin color and motion. The user can correct, if needed, the detected hand locations and pass the query to the system. Using Dynamic Time Warping their approach computes the similarity between the query sign and all the signs in the database. Their results suggest a 78% accuracy on the top-10 retrieved signs on a 1113 sign lexicon. While the accuracy rate is high enough, the user still needs to indicate the handedness feature (one- or two-handed) as well as the duration of the sign. Additionally, the data-set used in this study has been recorded under studio conditions posing the question of applicability on noisy real-life conditions on the video query.

Conly et al. (2015) have used Dynamic Time Warping to match a sign on an American Sign Language dictionary. Using Microsoft's Kinect they detect the hand positions and perform sign matching. Their results suggest an accuracy of 77.3% on the top-50 retrieved signs. A major advantage over Wang's et al. (2012) implementation is that this system does not require the intervention of the user.

Metaxas et al. (2018) have developed a framework that analyzes handshape, orientation, location, and motion trajectories to recognize 350 ASL signs. By passing the extracted features into Hidden Conditional Ordinal Random Fields (HCORF) they achieve a top-1 accuracy of 93.3% and a top-5 accuracy of 97.9%.

Vidalón and Martino (2016) have created a system for Brazilian Sign Language recognition using Dynamic Time Warping, a Nearest-Neighbor classifier and Kinect. On a data-set of 107 signs, they have reported an accuracy of approximately 98%. A major drawback of their results is the fact that their data-set is user-dependent.

The majority of the aforementioned studies use either a depth sensor or computer-vision techniques. These techniques primarily rely on color and motion detection algorithms, as feature extraction methods, which imposes additional problems. Such techniques can be prone to errors and most importantly require studio conditions in order to predict the required features such as the face and the hands. While such conditions can be true for the videos in a lexicon they cannot be assumed for the query videos. Searching a lexicon can be done in any possible space and lighting conditions, thus it is important that the technique used to capture the required features to be as much as inclusive as possible.

In 2017 Cao et al. (2017) presented a framework for multi-person 2D pose estimation, OpenPose. This framework can efficiently detect body, foot, hand and facial key-points from a simple RGB video or picture. Its high accuracy, performance and easy implementation make it the ideal framework to parse sign language and gestural videos. Its output consists of multiple json (or differently formatted) files containing all the pixel x, y coordinates of the body, hand and face joints. Most studies use OpenPose to pre-process the videos and use its output to further train or compare machine and deep learning models.

Schneider et al. (2019) have used OpenPose as well as DTW and Nearest-Neighbor algorithm to perform classification of six gestures. Their results suggested an accuracy of 77.4%. Most recently, Fragkiadakis et al. (2020) have used OpenPose and DTW to predict a sign recorded using a webcam from a 100 signs lexicon. Their method predicted the matching sign with an 87% and 74% accuracy at the top-10 and top-5 retrieved signs by using the path of the dominant hand's wrist.

This study extends on previous efforts for efficient sign ranking for sign language lexica by:

- Considering a far larger lexicon compared to previous efforts: 1200 signs in total
- Comparing four different techniques: Principal Component Analysis (PCA), Uniform Manifold Approximation and Projection for Dimension Reduction (UMAP), Dynamic Time Warping (DTW) and Euclidean distance
- Comparing three different skeletal joint combinations (upper body, dominant hand arm, dominant hand wrist)
- Exploring potential accuracy increase by adding more sign instances in the lexicon

An important difference from previous studies in search functionality for sign language dictionaries is that in our case we expect signers to not "properly" sign a particular sign. As Alonzo et al. (2019) discuss, it is possible that people would not remember exactly how a sign is performed, and as a result, they might sign it slightly differently. Thus it is expected that the matching sign would not be in the first retrieved sign result. This is precisely the reason why we tested our methodologies on a data-set that contains signs performed also by people with no or little experience in sign language. In most sign language data-sets used for sign language recognition tasks, signs are mostly performed by people familiar with sign languages. However, sign language lexica are intended also for people with little knowledge of sign language. As a result, high variability is expected when recording a sign.

Another limitation posed in our study is that sign language lexica do not often contain multiple instances of a particular sign. While various studies using deep learning techniques have shown high accuracy in predicting different signs (Li et al., 2020; Gökçe et al., 2020; Sincan and Keles, 2020; Hosain et al., 2021), they cannot be used in our case. These techniques often require vast amount of data in order to be trained which might not be available on all sign language lexica. Our main goal is to develop a system that can be easily used in any sign language lexicon regardless of the amount of data in it and most importantly the language itself. However, in this study, we explore the possibility of having a few additional sign instances in the lexicon and their potential benefit to successful sign retrieval.

3 Data-sets and Methods

In this section we describe the data pre-processing as well as the data-sets and methods used in this study.

3.1 Data Pre-processing and Normalization

OpenPose outputs x, y pixel coordinates for each predicted body and finger joint. These pixel coordinates are relative to the frame size and as a result it is important to normalize them to account for different positions in the frame. As all people in the data-set (both in participants' and lexicon's data) are expected to be in an upright position in front of the camera, rotational in-variance is omitted. The normalization process is the following: for each detected person in a frame, the neck key-point coordinates are subtracted from all the other key-points. Subsequently, all key point coordinates are being divided by the distance between the left and right shoulder key-point. Finally, a horizontal flip is applied when a participant is left-handed by calculating the average velocity of each hand's wrist. The overall normalization process is based on previous studies by Celebi et al. (2013), Schneider et al. (2019) and Fragkiadakis et al. (2020). Furthermore, all signs have been re-interpolated to 86 frames which is the mean sign length. Although it makes little difference to DTW's accuracy, equal length inputs make it easier to handle.

3.2 Data-sets

For this study we used the Ghanaian Sign Language lexicon (GSL) (Fragkiadakis et al., 2021; HANDS!Lab, 2020). This lexicon consists of 1200 signs from one signer and has been compiled for educational purposes to be used in a mobile application. A lot of studies in the sign language recognition field have used sign language data-sets from well documented sign languages with primarily signers with light skin tones. We have decided to apply our methodology in a sign language less documented and analyzed with computer vision and machine learning algorithms in order to further explore how these techniques can perform in such conditions.

In addition, the data gathered by Fragkiadakis et al. (2020) have been used to compare the different algorithms described in the next section. This data-set contains the data of ten participants. Each one of them performed the same 20 signs, from the original lexicon, in front of a webcam. The data of two participants have been discarded due to inconsistencies of OpenPose on recognizing their right-hand finger's and left arm joints.

We have decided to include in the lexicon the data from a random participant every time we tested the methodology. As the lighting conditions on the participants' videos were of poor quality, the predicted body joints by OpenPose had substantially more noise compared to the ones predicted on the lexicon's data. By extending the database with another participant's data, we introduced some noise to the otherwise non-noisy data-set. As a result, each participant's sign was compared with 1220 signs in our database (1200 from the GSL lexicon and 20 from another random participant). A complete overview of the participants' data-set and the apparatus used to gather the data can be found in Fragkiadakis's et al. (2020) study.

One of the main goals of this study is to find if and how different skeletal joints affect the accuracy of the algorithms. As a result, we have compiled 3 different data-sets per condition per participant's data. The first data-set contains the upper body joints as well as the dominant hand fingers joints' coordinates resulting in a $86 \times 29 \times 2$ (frames *by* skeletal joints *by* x, y coordinates) dimensionality per sign. Consecutively, the second data-set contains the dominant hand arm joints' coordinates (nose, neck, shoulder, elbow, wrist) resulting in a $86 \times 5 \times 2$ dimensionality per sign. Finally, the data-set regarding the dominant hand wrist data has a 86×2 dimensionality per sign.

3.3 Methods

The following section describes the methods and the four techniques used in this study.

3.3.1 Dimensionality Reduction

As described in the previous section, each sign in each compiled data-set can be seen as a multidimensional vector. To properly project it into the 2D space while still retaining most of the original information, we used two dimensionality reduction techniques.

The first technique applied is Principal Component Analysis (PCA). PCA is an orthogonal linear transformation that converts the data to a new frame of reference. PCA constructs Principal Components as linear combinations of the initial variables. These components are not correlated and most of the information within the introductory variables is compressed into the first components. By disposing the components with low information and taking into account the remaining ones as new variables, it allows for dimensionality reduction without loosing information. As a technique it has been widely used in the gestural as well as the sign language domain either as a visualization technique or as a pre-processing stage prior to other machine and deep learning stages (Gweth et al., 2012; Sawant and Kumbhar, 2014; Haque et al., 2019; Gao et al., 2021).

Furthermore, the Uniform Manifold Approximation and Projection for Dimension Reduction (UMAP) technique has been utilized. This method has been used instead of another popular dimensionality reduction technique called t-distributed stochastic neighbor embedding (T-sne) (Van der Maaten and Hinton, 2008). T-sne's inability to preserve the global structure of the data makes it unusable if distances between different clusters or points need to be calculated such as in our case (McInnes et al., 2018). In contrast, UMAP can better preserve both local and most of the global structure in the data allowing the calculation of distance metrics between clusters. Moreover, the lack of normalization in UMAP effectively reduces the time of computation of the high-dimensional graph.

In our study both PCA and UMAP have been used to reduce the dimensionality of each sign to a single x, y coordinate. Subsequently, we measured the euclidean distance between all the signs of the lexicon and the participants' signs. Accuracy for each participant's sign was measured based on whether the target sign was on the top-k shortest distant signs.

Furthermore, in order to validate the results produced by the UMAP algorithm in its ability to preserve the global distances of the data, we calculated their euclidean distances in the original high-dimensional space. This method has been used as a benchmark to compare the results of both PCA and UMAP.

3.3.2 Dynamic Time warping

In addition to the dimensionality reduction techniques described above, Dynamic Time Warping (DTW) has been used to measure the similarity between the different signs. Dynamic Time Warping is a dynamic programming based time series comparison algorithm to produce a distance metric between two inputs. It has been widely used in the speech recognition domain (Myers et al., 1980; Abdulla et al., 2003; Axelrod and Maison, 2004) as well as the gestural and sign language recognition fields as shown in Section 2.

In this study we utilize a DTW python implementation with open beginning and ending attributes by Giorgino (2009) and Tormene et al. (2009) which in a preliminary experiment produced better results compared to the previous DTW implementation by Fragkiadakis et al. (2020). Similarly, we used a median filter with radius $r = 3$ for smoothing the time series signals from the body joints.

Finally, the overall pipeline of the experiment can be seen in Figure 1.

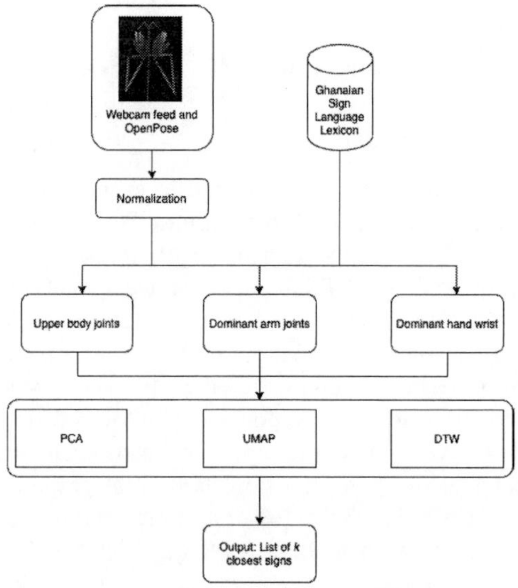

Figure 1: Pipeline of the overall study.

3.3.3 How many signs?

Many sign language lexica allow their users to submit their own versions of signs. As a result, different instances of the same sign can be stored in the database. One of our research questions is whether having multiple instances of each sign can potentially improve the accuracy of the algorithms. To verify that, we progressively added the 20 signs from other participants to the lexicon. Subsequently, we measured the average top-1 and top-10 accuracy for each algorithm and each skeletal condition.

Such information can be useful to sign language lexicographers when compiling sign language lexica. They can take advantage of crowd-sourcing material, contributing not only to the augmentation of their lexica but also to the accuracy of the models used for enhanced search functionality.

4 Results

Table 1 presents the overall accuracy for each of the skeletal conditions. Top-k refers to the number of signs a user must look up before finding a correct match. Accuracy indicates whether the target sign is present in the top-k retrieved signs and is averaged across all participants and all signs.

Highest accuracy is apparent at a top-50 level at 95% using the UMAP algorithm and the joints of the dominant hand arm. Furthermore, top-20 rank shows an adequate accuracy at 80% again using UMAP and the dominant hand arm coordinates. Figure 2 presents the visualizations of the UMAP algorithm for each of the skeletal condition for one participant. The results of the calculated euclidean distances on the original high-dimensional space show an adequate accuracy of approximately 68% at the top-50 rank in both dominant hand arm and wrist data-sets.

Principal component analysis (PCA) performed, on average, better using the wrist coordinates and showed the highest accuracy at the top-50 at approximately 41%.

DTW showed the highest accuracy at 79% at top-50 rank using the data of the dominant hand wrist and 77% using the dominant hand arm. On average, DTW had the best accuracy at

Skeletal condition	Upper body				Dominant hand arm				Dominant hand wrist			
Top-k	Top - 1	Top - 10	Top - 20	Top - 50	Top - 1	Top - 10	Top - 20	Top - 50	Top - 1	Top - 10	Top - 20	Top - 50
PCA	0.0375	0.1562	0.2187	0.325	0.025	0.1562	0.2125	0.3437	0.0187	0.1562	0.2125	0.4125
UMAP	0.1312	0.4125	0.6562	**0.6937**	0.0812	0.4375	**0.8**	**0.95**	0.1125	0.2562	0.3687	0.4575
DTW	**0.57**	**0.64**	**0.67**	0.687	**0.5188**	**0.65**	0.7188	0.7763	**0.5265**	**0.6562**	**0.7125**	**0.7937**
Euclidean distance	0.2125	0.4625	0.5325	0.6188	0.2625	0.5	0.6063	0.6938	0.1875	0.445	0.55	0.675

Table 1: Sign retrieval accuracy per algorithm (by row) on the three skeletal conditions based on the top-k retrieved signs (highest value per column in **bold**).

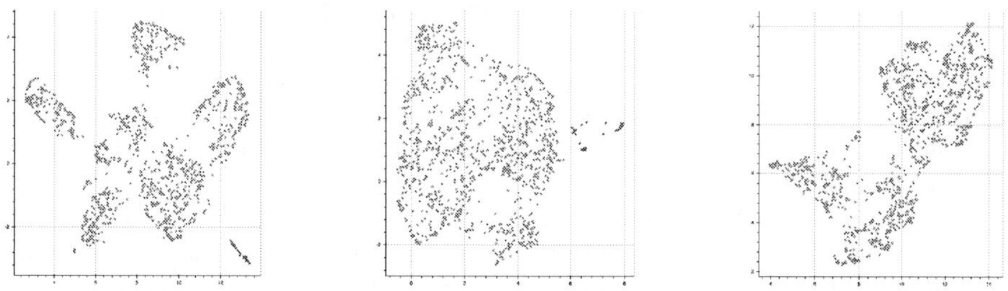

(a) upper body (b) dominant hand arm (c) dominant hand wrist

Figure 2: UMAP visualizations for one participant for the different skeletal conditions. With red are the signs of the participant and with blue the targeted signs.

around 70% at the top-20 retrieved signs regardless of the skeletal condition used, with a slight increase noticed using the dominant hand arm data.

Figure 3 presents the top-1 and top-10 accuracy levels using DTW and UMAP that have been computed by incrementally adding other participants' data in the lexicon. It can be observed that by adding more sign instances from 6 different participants, the accuracy reached a 90% level at the top-10 retrieved signs using DTW and the upper body and dominant hand wrist data. Furthermore, a raise of approximately 15% can be noticed at the top-1 rank on DTW using the upper body and dominant hand wrist joints by adding the data of just 2 participants (Figure 3a). On the other hand, UMAP did not show any adequate raise at the top-1 accuracy regardless of the added participants' data and skeletal condition. However, an increase, of approximately 35%, can be seen at the top-10 ranking level using the data of 2 participants (Figure 3b).

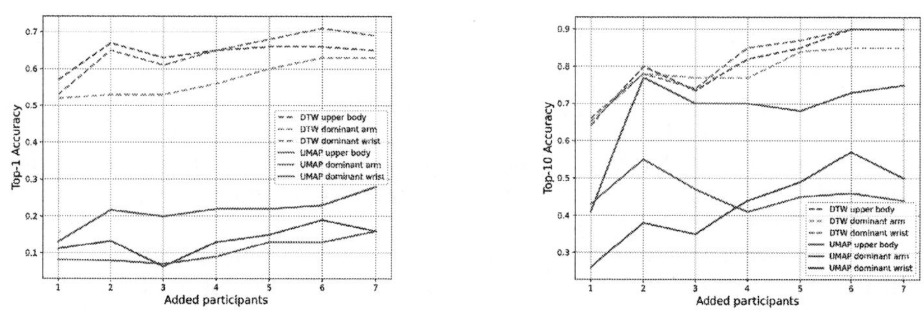

(a) Top-1 (b) Top-10

Figure 3: Top-1 (a) and Top-10 (b) accuracy using DTW and UMAP based on added participants' data in the lexicon.

5 Discussion

In this study we have investigated the use of OpenPose and four different implementations as distance metrics for an efficient ranking pipeline to retrieve matching signs from a sign language lexicon. The results demonstrated that, on a large vocabulary of 1200 signs, such a task can be achieved with an adequate accuracy rate using the Uniform Manifold Approximation and Projection for Dimension Reduction (UMAP) or Dynamic Time Warping (DTW) and the dominant arm joints' coordinates.

With regard to the visualizations produced by the UMAP algorithm, a few observations can be made. Firstly, by using the upper body joints UMAP produces discrete clusters. These clusters seem to reflect an abstract representation of the movement of each sign. This behavior has been observed also using the dominant hand arm coordinates, although it is more noticeable using all the upper-body joints. We have observed that signs that have similar movement but different handshapes are grouped close to each other.

However, special consideration needs to be made when viewing the visualizations produced by UMAP, especially the one using the upper body joints. The distances between the noticeable clusters, as well as their size relative to each other, do not hold any particular meaning. This is because of the use of local distances by the algorithm when constructing the graph. However, our results using the euclidean distances on the high-dimensional space suggest that UMAP preserves the original global distances.

Finally, it is worth mentioning that DTW performs equally well irrespective of the skeletal condition used at around 70% at the top-20 rank. Overall, it produces the most stable and consistent accuracy at the top-10 retrieved signs at around 65%. This accuracy level can be further raised reaching 90% by adding 6 more sign instances (from different signers) into the original lexicon. This attribute can be further explored by lexicographers by asking users of their lexica to submit their own versions of signs. This process can significantly boost the performance of DTW in its ability of retrieving the closest matching sign. A broad benefit of using such an algorithm is the fact that lexica compilers do not need to re-train any model if more signs or sign instances are added to their lexica.

In general, while our accuracy does not reach the ones reported by Schneider et al. (2019) and Fragkiadakis et al. (2020) (77.4% top-1 and 74% top-5 accuracy respectively) using similar algorithms and frameworks, our methods have been applied on a far larger lexicon (1200 signs instead of 6 and 100 respectively). As a result, we provide a better approximation on how these methods can actually be used in real world lexica.

6 Conclusions

To sum up, we have obtained satisfactory results demonstrating that UMAP and DTW, in combination with the pre-trained pose estimation framework OpenPose, can be used as an efficient sign ranking and retrieval system. Our method can effectively be applied to any sign language lexicon without any training process involved.

To the best of our knowledge, this is the first study using UMAP as a dimensionality reduction technique within the sign language domain and showcasing the strength of such algorithm compared to other implementations.

Future work will focus on exploring additional deep learning implementations for an efficient handshape and pose recognition. Their use, as well as supplementary hyper-parameter optimization for the techniques used in this study, could lead to an increase in accuracy. Whilst as we argued that for the availability of dictionaries it will be good to focus on zero training approaches, in future work we intend to run comparative analysis to understand the impact of training based approaches on performance. We propose that further research should also be undertaken in order to assess the application of our method on different datasets and languages. On a wider level, the techniques used in this study could be further explored to measure variation in different sign languages. The results from the use of UMAP and DTW on a large vocabulary suggest that these techniques might be well suited for variation measurement tasks, broadening their use beyond the search functionality for sign language lexica.

References

Abdulla, W. H., Chow, D., and Sin, G. (2003). Cross-words reference template for dtw-based speech recognition systems. In *Proceedings of the TENCON Conference on Convergent Technologies for Asia-Pacific Region*, volume 4, pages 1576–1579. Allied Publishers Pvt. Ltd.

Alonzo, O., Glasser, A., and Huenerfauth, M. (2019). Effect of automatic sign recognition performance on the usability of video-based search interfaces for sign language dictionaries. In *Proceedings of the 21st International ACM SIGACCESS Conference on Computers and Accessibility*, pages 56–67. ACM.

Axelrod, S. and Maison, B. (2004). Combination of hidden markov models with dynamic time warping for speech recognition. In *Proceedings of the 2004 IEEE International Conference on Acoustics, Speech, and Signal Processing*, volume 1, pages I–173–6, Montreal, Que., Canada. IEEE.

Cao, Z., Simon, T., Wei, S.-E., and Sheikh, Y. (2017). Realtime multi-person 2d pose estimation using part affinity fields. In *Proceedings of the 2017 IEEE Conference on Computer Vision and Pattern Recognition (CVPR)*, pages 1302–1310. IEEE.

Celebi, S., Aydin, A. S., Temiz, T. T., and Arici, T. (2013). Gesture recognition using skeleton data with weighted dynamic time warping. In *Proceedings of the 2013 International Joint Conference on Computer Vision, Imaging, and Computer Graphics Theory and Applications (VISAPP)*, pages 620–625.

Conly, C., Zhang, Z., and Athitsos, V. (2015). An integrated RGB-D system for looking up the meaning of signs. In *Proceedings of the 8th ACM International Conference on PErvasive Technologies Related to Assistive Environments (PETRA)*, pages 1–8. ACM Press.

Fragkiadakis, M., Nyst, V., and Nyarko, M. (2021). Ghanaian Sign Language Lexicon. `https://zenodo.org/record/4533753`.

Fragkiadakis, M., Nyst, V., and van der Putten, P. (2020). Signing as input for a dictionary query: matching signs based on joint positions of the dominant hand. In *Proceedings of the 9th Workshop on the Representation and Processing of Sign Languages*, pages 69–74. European Language Resources Association.

Gao, Y., Xue, C., Wang, R., and Jiang, X. (2021). Chinese fingerspelling recognition via gray-level co-occurrence matrix and fuzzy support vector machine. *EAI Endorsed Transactions on e-Learning*, 7(20):1–13.

Giorgino, T. (2009). Computing and visualizing dynamic time warping alignments in R: the dtw package. *Journal of statistical Software*, 31(7):1–24.

Gökçe, Ç., Özdemir, O., Kındıroğlu, A. A., and Akarun, L. (2020). Score-level multi cue fusion for sign language recognition. In *Computer Vision – ECCV 2020 Workshops*, pages 294–309. Springer International Publishing.

Gweth, Y. L., Plahl, C., and Ney, H. (2012). Enhanced continuous sign language recognition using PCA and neural network features. In *Proceedings of the 2012 IEEE Conference on Computer Vision and Pattern Recognition (CVPR)*, pages 55–60. IEEE.

HANDS!Lab (2020). Ghanaian Sign Language app. https://play.google.com/store/apps/details?id=com.ljsharp.gsldictionary&hl=es_US.

Haque, P., Das, B., and Kaspy, N. N. (2019). Two-handed bangla sign language recognition using principal component analysis (pca) and knn algorithm. In *Proceedings of the 2019 International Conference on Electrical, Computer and Communication Engineering (ECCE)*, pages 1–4. IEEE.

Hosain, A. A., Santhalingam, P. S., Pathak, P., Rangwala, H., and Kosecka, J. (2021). Hand pose guided 3d pooling for word-level sign language recognition. In *Proceedings of the IEEE/CVF Winter Conference on Applications of Computer Vision (WACV)*, pages 3429–3439.

Li, D., Rodriguez, C., Yu, X., and Li, H. (2020). Word-level deep sign language recognition from video: A new large-scale dataset and methods comparison. In *Proceedings of the IEEE/CVF Winter Conference on Applications of Computer Vision (WACV)*, pages 1459–1469.

McInnes, L., Healy, J., and Melville, J. (2018). Umap: Uniform manifold approximation and projection for dimension reduction. *arXiv preprint arXiv:1802.03426*.

Metaxas, D., Dilsizian, M., and Neidle, C. (2018). Linguistically-driven framework for computationally efficient and scalable sign recognition. In *Proceedings of the 11th International Conference on Language Resources and Evaluation (LREC)*, Miyazaki, Japan. European Language Resources Association (ELRA).

Myers, C., Rabiner, L., and Rosenberg, A. (1980). Performance tradeoffs in dynamic time warping algorithms for isolated word recognition. *IEEE Transactions on Acoustics, Speech, and Signal Processing*, 28(6):623–635.

Sawant, S. N. and Kumbhar, M. S. (2014). Real time sign language recognition using pca. In *Proceedings of the 2014 IEEE International Conference on Advanced Communications, Control and Computing Technologies*, pages 1412–1415. IEEE.

Schneider, P., Memmesheimer, R., Kramer, I., and Paulus, D. (2019). Gesture recognition in RGB videos using human body keypoints and dynamic time warping. In *RoboCup 2019: Robot World Cup XXIII*, pages 281–293. Springer International Publishing.

Sincan, O. M. and Keles, H. Y. (2020). Autsl: A large scale multi-modal turkish sign language dataset and baseline methods. *IEEE Access*, 8:181340–181355.

Tormene, P., Giorgino, T., Quaglini, S., and Stefanelli, M. (2009). Matching incomplete time series with dynamic time warping: an algorithm and an application to post-stroke rehabilitation. *Artificial Intelligence in Medicine*, 45(1):11–34.

Van der Maaten, L. and Hinton, G. (2008). Visualizing data using t-SNE. *Journal of machine learning research*, 9(11).

Vidalón, J. E. Y. and Martino, J. M. D. (2016). Brazilian sign language recognition using kinect. In *Lecture Notes in Computer Science*, pages 391–402. Springer International Publishing.

Wang, H., Stefan, A., Moradi, S., Athitsos, V., Neidle, C., and Kamangar, F. (2012). A system for large vocabulary sign search. In *Trends and Topics in Computer Vision*, pages 342–353. Springer, Berlin, Heidelberg.

Zwitserlood, I. (2010). Sign language lexicography in the early 21st century and a recently published dictionary of sign language of the netherlands. *International Journal of Lexicography*, 23(4):443–476.

The myth of signing avatars

Rosalee Wolfe Rosalee.Wolfe@athenarc.gr
Institute for Language and Speech Processing, Athena RC, Greece
John C. McDonald jmcdonald@cs.depaul.edu
School of Computing, DePaul University, Chicago, USA
Eleni Efthimiou eleni_e@athenarc.gr
Institute for Language and Speech Processing, Athena RC, Greece
Evita Fontinea evita@athenarc.gr
Institute for Language and Speech Processing, Athena RC, Greece
Frankie Picron frankie.picron@eud.eu
European Union of the Deaf, Brussels, Belgium
Davy Van Landuyt davy.van.landuyt@eud.eu
European Union of the Deaf, Brussels, Belgium
Tina Sioen tina.sioen@eud.eu
European Union of the Deaf, Brussels, Belgium
Annelies Braffort annelies.braffort@lisn.upsaclay.fr
Laboratoire Interdisciplinaire des Sciences du Numérique, Orsay, France
Michael Filhol michael.filhol@lisn.upsaclay.fr
Laboratoire Interdisciplinaire des Sciences du Numérique, Orsay, France
Sarah Ebling ebling@cl.uzh.ch
Department of Computational Linguistics, University of Zurich, Switzerland
Thomas Hanke thomas.hanke@uni-hamburg.de
Institut für Deutsche Gebärdensprache, Universität Hamburg, Germany
Verena Krausneker verena.krausneker@univie.ac.at
Institut für Sprachwissenschaft, Universität Wien, Vienna, Austria

Abstract

Development of automatic translation between signed and spoken languages has lagged behind the development of automatic translation between spoken languages, but it is a common misperception that extending machine translation techniques to include signed languages should be a straightforward process. A contributing factor is the lack of an acceptable method for displaying sign language apart from interpreters on video. This position paper examines the challenges of displaying a signed language as a target in automatic translation, analyses the underlying causes and suggests strategies to develop display technologies that are acceptable to sign language communities.

1. Introduction

Deaf sign language users around the world face continual challenges in daily interaction with hearing, non-signing populations. The gold standard for translating between signed and spoken languages[1] are certified sign language interpreters who are essential to facilitating communication for education, healthcare, and legal consultation among other situations. However, many transactions in daily living consist of short conversations over a hotel desk, at a store counter or in an office foyer. These interactions are so limited in scope and duration that hiring a qualified interpreter would be prohibitively expensive or quite unnecessary, or even impossible because in most countries there is a shortage of qualified interpreters. In such situations, an automatic translation system between spoken and signed language would ease communication barriers and improve inclusivity. For technology of this sort to be useful, it must display sign language in a way that is acceptable to members of the sign language community.

To be effective, an automated translation system or machine translation system must be able to produce legible, grammatically, and phonologically and phonetically correct, acceptable utterances in a desired target language with minimal or no human involvement. Researchers have made significant progress in translating between high-resource languages that have a written form and some have suggested that automatic translation has achieved human parity in some domains (Hassan, et al., 2018).

Progress in translating between signed and spoken languages has lagged significantly in comparison. Traditionally, this task has been conceived as one of text-to-text translation, involving written representations of sign languages. Since sign languages have no widely accepted written form, an additional required step in going from a spoken language to a sign language is that of displaying signed languages in their natural moving form, in the visual modality (Ebling, 2016). This position paper examines the challenges of displaying signed language as a target in automatic translation, analyses the underlying impediments and suggests strategies to develop display technologies that are acceptable to deaf sign language users.

2. Background

Sign languages are distinct from their surrounding spoken languages. For example, in France, many deaf persons have Langue des Signes Française (LSF), not French, as their preferred language. Since French is a second language to them, even its written form poses a barrier. Many researchers have noted that written language poses barriers to members of the Deaf communities (Traxler, 2000; Gutjahr, 2006; Hennies, 2010; Konrad, 2011).

Deaf sign language users consider themselves members of a minority group, with a distinct language, culture, and shared experiences, rather than as simply persons with a disability (De Meulder, Krausneker, Turner, & Conama, 2019). They continually struggle with the reality that policy makers in governmental departments, educational institutions and health care agencies consist primarily of hearing people who are not familiar with the values, goals and concerns of sign language communities (Branson & Miller, 1998). As a result, there is a history of disenfranchisement which adds a barrier of distrust to the barrier of language that exists between deaf and hearing communities. At present, current technology claiming to translate between spoken and signed languages are not viewed favourably by sign language communities. Rather, the technology is often perceived as a ploy to replace human interpreters (World Federation of the Deaf, 2018; European Union of the Deaf, 2018), or even as cultural appropriation by predominantly hearing researchers, who do not always have linguistic knowledge of these languages, and often have little connection with sign language communities (Erard, 2017).

[1] The term *spoken language* refers to any language that is not signed, whether represented as speech or as text.

Linguists have noted that as long as avatars are only capable of artificial and flawed language, they are very likely to be counterproductive. (Austrian Association of Applied Linguistics, 2019).

This scepticism and often downright hostility towards automatic translation systems is exacerbated by the generally poor quality of their sign language (Sayers, et al., 2021). To date these have exhibited robotic movement and are mostly unable to reproduce all of the multi-modal articulation mechanisms necessary to be legible. They are comparable to early speech synthesis systems which featured robotic-sounding voices that chained words together with little regard to coarticulation and no attention to prosody.

3. Quality of the target language

Just as with text-to-text translation applications, users will judge the quality of the application by the quality of its output to the target language. The same is true when the target language is signed. Poor-quality signing is difficult to understand, just as poor-quality speech synthesis or egregious misspellings are difficult to understand. It undermines the viewer's confidence in the quality of the translation. Worse, poor quality signing alienates the sign language community. Being forced to struggle with the poor signing is no better than being forced to lip read or use captions in the second language.

This is simply more evidence that reconfirms a continuing disenfranchisement. For these reasons, quality of the ultimate signed language display must be given highest priority in a spoken to signed translation system. The motion should be indistinguishable from that of a human signing the same utterance. This visual Turing Test should be the ultimate goal of any sign language display.

4. Sign language in automatic translation services

Among the challenges to acceptable sign language display as part of an automatic translation system, three issues stand out. These are 1) the difference of modalities between signed and spoken languages 2) the representation used to characterize sign languages and 3) the development of the technology required to display sign languages.

4.1. Modality

The modality of sign languages differs markedly from that of spoken languages, which utilize the vocal apparatus for production, and hearing for reception. Spoken languages use visible communicative behaviours like gestures as well, but listeners can comprehend audio-only sources. In contrast, signed languages use only visible actions for production, and vision for reception. Whereas speech utilizes a single vibrating column of air for producing utterances, signed languages use the configuration and movement of multiple body parts concurrently, including hands with all the fingers, head, face, eyes, and torso.

All sign languages have linguistic processes that are not linearly ordered. For example, in American Sign Language (ASL) the appearance of pursed lips in conjunction with the sign SMOOTH intensifies the degree of smoothness. In signed language, layers of processes ranging from the phonological to the prosodic can co-occur (Crasborn, 2006). Co-occurrence is a more general term than synchronized or simultaneous, as co-occurring events do not necessarily start or end at the same time, but they overlap in their duration.

Although there are many discrete lexical items in signed languages, much information is conveyed through forms with infinite variability and depiction, unlike fixed dictionary signs. A case in point are classifiers, which represent general categories or "classes" of objects. They can be used to describe the size and shape of an object, and they can also represent how an object moves or is utilized. Through the use of classifiers, a signer can describe a scenario with few discrete lexical items. The signer creates an image in space. This is not simply an informal gesture as there are well-documented linguistic rules governing classifier usage (Lepic & Occhino, 2018). These are evocative, not necessarily iconic, and are extremely powerful. In a story about a motorcycle ride (Dudis, 2004), a signer can use an instrument classifier to indicate that the rider is revving the engine and a vehicle classifier to show the rider driving away on a hilly highway (Figure 1).

The motorcyclist driving up a hill

Figure 1. Classifier usage (Dudis, 2004).

The presence of multiple articulators that can co-occur and classifier usage are examples of the stark difference between signed and spoken languages. For these reasons, it is essential to avoid the trap of casting the problem of signed/spoken translation as a case of simply retrieving lexical items or phrasal units from a dictionary and concatenating them.

4.2. Representation

The second of the three challenges is the question of representation. Languages commonly processed by automatic translation systems have a written form. Signed languages do not. They are languages and cultures that have been preserved and transmitted from generation to generation by "hand to eye to hand". Determining a standard transcription/annotation system that can capture all of the linguistic information contained in a signed message is still an open question. A linear stream of glosses, even with accompanying superscript strings to indicate prosody and syntax (Adamo-Villani & Wilbur, 2015), does not contain the entire semantic content of a signed utterance, in particular the depicting and spatialized linguistic structures.

This is not analogous to the difference between reading printed text on a page and witnessing an actor perform the text. Less information is captured in a gloss stream than is conveyed in written text. A hearing person may argue that not all features of articulation are captured in a printed sentence of a spoken language, such as speed of delivery, but in languages where adverbs are not necessarily expressed as separate lexical items, the lack of a speed indication is losing semantic information, not just performance information.

4.3. Sign language display

The third challenge is the display of a sign language when it is the target. The most commonly used strategy for this purpose is avatar technology. Three-dimensional avatars have the advantages of consistency and flexibility. When recording a human signer with traditional video, special care must be taken to ensure consistency of the studio set up and the appearance of the signer between recording sessions. This requires additional time and money. When using an avatar, the lighting and camera set up can be fixed; the clothing can be chosen by the viewer as can the hair and makeup. No additional resources are required to ensure consistency.

In addition, avatars have the advantage of flexibility through the use of animation techniques. They can display co-occurring linguistic processes. Proper application of coarticulation can provide smooth transitions and can inflect signs according to syntactic rules. These properties are necessary for a translation system to produce novel utterances.

Avatars also have flexibility in appearance. They can be easily adapted to look like the shape of the original speaker/source, like a presenter or a cartoon character or a movie character. This flexibility in appearance can also anonymize a signer, so that the signer's identity will remain hidden.

Another advantage of this type of anonymization of content is that it covers one of the key properties of written language, which is inherently more anonymous than a live performance that is spoken or signed. With an anonymously presented avatar, content can be communicated without knowing the person who expressed it.

5. The promise and mythology of avatars

Given that there is a century's worth of development in animation, and nearly half that supporting video game technology, it would be tempting to dismiss the question of using avatars to display sign languages as a solved problem. However, a closer analysis shows that there are still significant challenges yet to be fully addressed.

Animation, the precursor to avatar technology, is powerfully communicative. Animation artists abstract and emphasize the salient features of a character for greater audience appeal and engagement. Simplification of a character's appearance is vital to maximizing emotional impact. This is the reason that the eyes of Disney cartoon characters are twice the size of those of a human and spaced more widely apart.

However, the requirements for sign language display are different from those for portraying cartoon characters. Beyond communicative power, display of sign language requires precision. It must adhere more closely to physical reality. For example, the hands of animation characters such as Mickey Mouse or Homer Simpson have only three fingers. For a hearing audience, this is perfectly acceptable, but three fingers aren't enough to distinguish between the fingerspelled letter W and the number 4 (Figure 2). Another consideration is that while character animation effectively uses the face and body to express emotion, the facial animation is typically at a lower quality than what would be required to portray a sign language legibly.

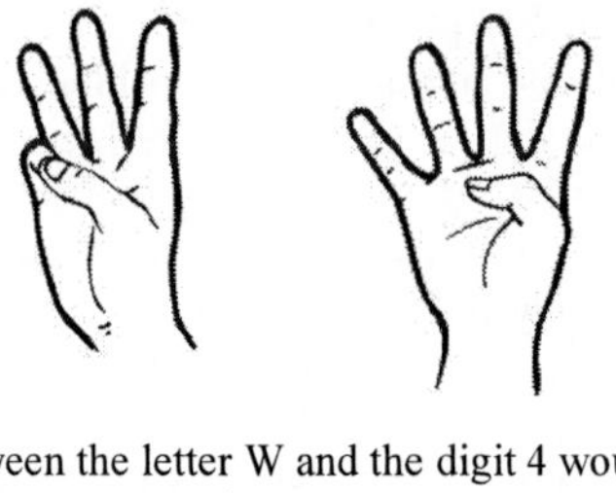

Figure 2. The difference between the letter W and the digit 4 would disappear in a three-fingered character.

Several ground-breaking animations have received attention and praise from sign language communities (Stewart, 2008; Fumdación Fesord CV, 2007). These were manually created by artists with the assistance of motion capture. The artists create underlying natural processes of coordinated muscle action, coarticulation at a biomechanical level and ambient movement. While creating the animation the artists are continually checking whether the animation draft effectively communicates the intended message and editing the draft when there are flaws. However, animations are intended for playback only and are not extensible without manual intervention. Once completed, they are archived, and without additional manual editing cannot be utilized for generating new utterances. In short, animations are not created in real time and are not interactive.

In contrast, video game characters move in response to player input in real time and are highly interactive. Thus, using video game technology might seem like an expedient approach to sign language display for a translation system. However, many game players continue to comment on the poor quality of the game characters. This is due to the effect of the uncanny valley (Tinwell, 2014). If a character appears more human-like, viewers expect the character to behave in a more human-like manner. But because the character's motion cannot be refined and edited by human animators before it is displayed, the results are unsatisfying. As explained by a professional animator (Trentskiroonie, 2015),

> For something like film or television, I could create a kickass animation of a monster jumping off a building and landing on the street below, but to do the same thing in a game, the movement has to be broken up into separate parts. This is because he probably won't do the exact same action every time. There may be buildings of different heights in the game, so I can't hard-code the height of the jump into the animation. I have to create an initial jump animation, then an idle hang-time animation to play while he's in the air, and then a landing animation. The programmer then strings the jump, hang-time, and landing together and decides the timing and trajectory of the hang-time part procedurally. ... That takes artistic control away from the animator and can result in some fugly animation.

Unfortunately, a "fugly" motion on a sign language avatar can destroy the legibility and even the meaning of the message, thus making the avatar bothersome or even useless for a deaf sign language user. Finally, the representation of signed languages through avatars will have an effect on the hearing perception of these minority languages. Hearing viewers should not be confronted with "fugly" signed texts and be misled into thinking that it is real sign language in all its beauty and richness.

The analysis of the requirements for a sign language avatar shows that it must have the expressivity of manual animation but the flexibility of a video game character. These two requirements are in conflict. It is still an open question as to how to reconcile these goals.

6. Moving forward

The establishment of a set of best practices would be a substantive step toward the development of better sign language displays in automatic translation systems, but it cannot happen without a mutual collaboration with sign language stakeholders (Tupi, 2019). Deaf leadership is vital for the establishment of a validated methodology for user evaluation of avatar technology. Once created and reviewed, the methodology should be made publicly available to all researchers working in this area. Currently in Austria, there is a small research project aiming to create a Best Practice Protocol for the use of signing avatars (Krausneker, 2021).

This is consistent with the World Federation of the Deaf's position paper on Sign Language Work (World Federation of the Deaf, 2014).

> The WFD considers exclusion of Deaf Community and their national organizations from sign language work ... a violation of the linguistic human rights of deaf people. Decisions regarding sign languages should always remain within the linguistic community, in this case deaf people.

Best practice for reviewing research papers would include an awareness of the multidisciplinary qualification required. It is not enough to know about machine translation. Reviewers must also be aware of sign language linguistics, the deaf experience and previous work in sign language machine translation.

When reporting on an advance in sign language avatar technology, researchers should include a sample of the sign language produced by the technique outlined in a paper. Since the sample would necessarily contain motion, it could either take the form of a media file in a commonly available format such as MPEG-4, or a web application available online. Conference organizers and journal editors need to collaborate with academic and professional organizations to archive media accompanying research papers.

7. Conclusion

"Together, we are strong." -- Lutz König, Hamburg, 14 November 2017

Together, machine translation (MT) researchers, sign language linguists and the deaf sign language community have the potential to form powerful partnerships to educate policy makers (Bragg, et al., 2019). Ideally, Deaf professionals should be educated, supported, and actively sought to include in sign language relevant research projects.

To hearing researchers: Get to know members of sign language communities and learn about deaf culture.

- Take a class in the national sign language of your country. You already know several spoken languages -- why not discover an entirely new world? Or if you don't feel you have time,
- Go to a deaf event -- see a play in sign language, go to a deaf trade show.
- When writing grant proposals that include work relevant for sign languages, include the local and/or national deaf community. Most countries in the world have a National Association of the Deaf. Include budget for interpreters.
- Listen. Just because an idea or a result is incredibly appealing to an MT researcher does not mean that it will be useful or welcomed within the sign language community. Take feedback seriously and act on it.

Through exchange of ideas and concerns, the sign language community can inform MT researchers about their priorities, and MT researchers can clarify the capabilities and limitations of today's technologies. A clear understanding of priorities, expectations, potentials, and limitations will move the state of the art closer to realization of better inclusivity.

Acknowledgments

This work is supported in part by the EASIER (Intelligent Automatic Sign Language Translation) Project. EASIER has received funding from the European Union's Horizon 2020 research and innovation programme, grant agreement n° 101016982.

Bibliography

Adamo-Villani, N., & Wilbur, R. B. (2015). ASL-Pro: American sign language animation with prosodic elements. *International Conference on Universal Access in Human-Computer Interaction,* (pp. 307–318).

Austrian Association of Applied Linguistics. (2019, August). *Position Paper on Automated Translations and Signing Avatars.* Récupéré sur verbal; Verband für Angewandte Linguistik Österreich: https://www.verbal.at/stellungnahmen/Position_Paper-Avatars_verbal_2019.pdf

Bragg, D., Koller, O., Bellard, M., Berke, L., Boudreault, P., Braffort, A., . . . others. (2019). Sign language recognition, generation, and translation: An interdisciplinary perspective. *The 21st International ACM SIGACCESS Conference on Computers and Accessibility,* (pp. 16–31).

Branson, J., & Miller, D. (1998). Nationalism and the linguistic rights of Deaf communities: Linguistic imperialism and the recognition and development of sign languages. *Journal of Sociolinguistics, 2,* 3–34.

Crasborn, O. A. (2006). Nonmanual structures in sign language. Dans K. Brown (Éd.), *Encyclopedia of Language and Linguistics* (éd. 2nd, pp. 668-672). Oxford: Elsevier.

De Meulder, M., Krausneker, V., Turner, G., & Conama, J. B. (2019). Sign language communities. Dans G. Hogan-Burn, & B. O'Rourke (Éd.), *The Palgrave Handbook of Minority Languages and Communities* (pp. 207-232). London: Palgrave Macmillan.

Dudis, P. G. (2004). Body partitioning and real-space blends. *Cognitive Linguistics, 15*(2), 223-238.

Ebling, S. (2016). *Automatic Translation from German to Synthesized Swiss German Sign Language.* Ph.D. dissertation, University of Zurich.

Erard, M. (2017, November 9). *Why sign-language gloves don't help deaf people.* Récupéré sur The Atlantic: https://www.theatlantic.com/technology/archive/2017/11/why-sign-language-gloves-dont-help-deaf-people/545441/

European Union of the Deaf. (2018, October 26). *Accessibility of information and communication.* Récupéré sur European Union of the Deaf : https://www.eud.eu/about-us/eud-position-paper/accessibility-information-and-communication/

Fundación Fesord CV. (2007, Jan 26). *World Federation of the Deaf 2007.* Récupéré sur youtube: https://www.youtube.com/watch?v=wW2KBXrPEdM

Gutjahr, A. E. (2006). *Lesekompetenz Gehörloser: Ein Forschungsüberblick.* Ph.D. dissertation.

Hassan, H., Aue, A., Chen, C., Chowdhary, V., Clark, J., Federmann, C., . . . Zhou, M. (2018, Mar 15). *Achieving Human Parity on Automatic Chinese to English News Translation.* Récupéré sur Microsoft.com: https://www.microsoft.com/en-us/research/uploads/prod/2018/03/final-achieving-human.pdf

Hennies, J. (2010). Lesekompetenz gehörloser und schwerhöriger SchülerInnen Ein Beitrag zur empirischen Bildungsforschung in der Hörgeschädigtenpädagogik.

Johnson, M., Schuster, M., Le, Q. V., Krikun, M., Wu, Y., Chen, Z., . . . others. (2017). Google's multilingual neural machine translation system: Enabling zero-shot translation. *Transactions of the Association for Computational Linguistics, 5*, 339–351.

Konrad, R. (2011). *Die lexikalische Struktur der Deutschen Gebärdensprache im Spiegel empirischer Fachgebärdenlexikographie.* Gunter Narr Verlag.

Krausneker, V. (2021). *Avatars and sign languages: Developing a best practice protocol on quality in accessibility.* Récupéré sur University of Vienna: https://avatar-bestpractice.univie.ac.at/

Lepic, R., & Occhino, C. (2018). A construction morphology approach to sign language analysis. Dans *The construction of words* (pp. 141–172). Springer.

Sayers, D., Sousa-Silva, R., Höhn, S., Ahmedi, L., Allkivi-Metsoja, K., Anastasiou, D., . . . others. (2021). *The dawn of the human-machine era: A forecast of new and emerging language technologies.* Récupéré sur LITHME: https://lithme.eu/wp-content/uploads/2021/05/The-dawn-of-the-human-machine-era-a-forecast-report-2021-final.pdf

Stewart, J. (2008, July 21). *The Forest - A story in ASL.* Récupéré sur youtube: https://www.youtube.com/watch?v=oUclQ10BsH8

Tinwell, A. (2014). *The uncanny valley in games and animation.* CRC Press.

Traxler, C. B. (2000). The Stanford achievement test: National norming and performance standards for deaf and hard-of-hearing students. *Journal of deaf studies and deaf education, 5*, 337–348.

Trentskiroonie. (2015). *Let's talk about Animation Quality!* Récupéré sur reddit.com: https://www.reddit.com/r/truegaming/comments/2x4fqy/lets_talk_about_animation_quality/

Tupi, E. (2019). Sign language rights in the framework of the Council of Europe and its member states. *Sign language rights in the framework of the Council of Europe and its member states*. Helsinki: Ministry for Foreign Affairs of Finland.

World Federation of the Deaf. (2014, February 19). *WFD statement of sign language work.* Récupéré sur World Federation of the Deaf: http://wfdeaf.org/wp-content/uploads/2016/11/WFD-statement-sign-language-work.pdf

World Federation of the Deaf. (2018, March 14). *WFD and WASLI statement of use of signing avatars.* Récupéré sur World Federation of the Deaf: https://wfdeaf.org/news/resources/wfd-wasli-statement-use-signing-avatars/

AVASAG: A German Sign Language Translation System for Public Services

Fabrizio Nunnari[3] **Judith Bauerdiek**[1] **Lucas Bernhard**[4] **Cristina España-Bonet**[3]
Corinna Jäger[6] **Amelie Unger**[2] **Kristoffer Waldow**[5] **Sonja Wecker**[6]
Elisabeth André[4] **Stephan Busemann**[3] **Christian Dold**[1] **Arnulph Fuhrmann**[5]
Patrick Gebhard[3] **Yasser Hamidullah**[3] **Marcel Hauck**[1] **Yvonne Kossel**[6]
Martin Misiak[5] **Dieter Wallach**[2] **Alexander Stricker**[1]

[1]Charamel GmbH, Cologne, Germany (Project-Coordinator)
[2]Ergosign GmbH, Hamburg, Germany
[3]German Research Center for Artificial Intelligence (DFKI), Saarland Informatics Campus D3.2, Saarbrücken, Germany
[4]Human-Centered Artificial Intelligence, University of Augsburg, Germany
[5]TH, Köln, Germany
[6]yomma GmbH, Hamburg, Germany

Abstract

This paper presents an overview of AVASAG; an ongoing applied-research project developing a text-to-sign-language translation system for public services. We describe the scientific innovation points (geometry-based SL-description, 3D animation and video corpus, simplified annotation scheme, motion capture strategy) and the overall translation pipeline.

1 Introduction

The development of software solutions able to translate (bi-directionally) from spoken language to sign-language (SL) has received a lot of attention during the last years. In Europe, the involvement of the public institutions in such line of research culminated with the funding, under the H2020 program, of two 3-year long research projects, namely EASIER [12] and SignON [13, 15].

In this paper, we present the architecture of project AVASAG [11] (Avatar-basierter Sprachassistent zur automatisierten Gebärdenübersetzung = Avatar-based speaking assistant for the automated translation of sign language), which is a project funded by the German ministry for education and research (BMBF) aiming at deploying a commercial system able to automatically translate text to sign language in various domains of public services (e.g., announcements for railway stations, airports, harbors, and hygiene warnings). The implementation choices are driven by the following requirements and constraints:

1. The system is devoted to off-line translation services. Hence, translation does not need to be necessarily in real-time, but rather offer the possibility to human operators (likely trained interpreters) to finalize the animation through manual editing, and approve it before delivery;
2. The avatar animation will be tuned to maximize comprehensibility, while at the same time maintaining a sufficient level of acceptance in terms of naturalness of the animation. This

can be seen as the compromise set to initial synthetic voices used for public services;

3. In order to approach the market within a reasonable time frame, the project focuses on realizing at first well recognized forms of inflection of lexical signs (e.g., sign relocation, interrogative forms, role shifts, classifiers), but still open to the realization of more creative iconic gestures in future extensions;
4. The system is engineered to scale with time as new signs are added to its vocabulary to support more application domains.

From a scientific point of view, the project aims at the following innovation points.

First, the project is developing a translation system that goes beyond classic symbolic representation of SL. Existing *SL-descriptions* range from mere un-contextualized GLOSSES, to more sophisticated formats specifying hand (shape, orientation, location, trajectory) and facial movements (e.g., Stokoe [16], HamNoSys [5]). This gives the opportunity to human operators for the corrections of sentences when the text-to-SL-description fails. However, compared to data-driven approaches, animations driven by SL symbolic descriptors are generally judged as generating non-believable unnatural animations (see [10] for an overview). On the other hand, recent end-to-end data-driven approaches are moving towards the generation of 3D sign pose sequences [14] that could be used to animate an avatar from a kinematic level, but hinders the possibility of a manual correction of the translation result.

In this project, we try to merge the advantages of data-driven animation, which leads to more natural looking results, while leaving the capability of post-translation manual correction. Given a vocabulary of motion captured signs, the inflection of signs within the context of a sentence will be realized by transforming a sign data using: i) non-rigid 3D transformation (translation, rotation, scaling, shearing) of the hand trajectories and torso movement, ii) corrective blend-shapes on the facial animation, and iii) time-warping functions controlling the dynamic of the execution. All of those inflection transformations are driven by numerical parameters that can be manipulated by a human through the use of "3D gizmos" in a dedicated editing GUI.

As an advantage with respect to performing end-to-end translation (directly from text to avatar animation data), predicting only inflection parameters significantly reduces the size of the target output, thus likely allowing for the preparation of accurate models with much less training material.

Second, the project will deliver to the scientific community, with public unrestricted access, a **corpus of sentences** with parallel data whose entries are composed of:

- The ***text of the sentence*** in natural language (both in the host language and in its English translation);
- a ***GLOSS transcription*** of the sentences using the philosophy of the gloss-ID [6];
- the ***3D motion capture (MoCap) data*** of the corresponding SL translation, captured in a high-class motion capture studio, for full body, hands, and facial animation;
- ***Full-HD*** video of the interpreter during the same motion capture session, hence synchronized at frame level with the 3D MoCap data;
- the ***annotation*** of the sentence videos on different tiers (see the third innovation point for details) performed with a cross-check procedure by native deaf and SL interpreters;
- the ***inflection parameters***, i.e., the values for the (3D) transformation inflecting the signs.

In addition, the corpus will be paired with a **vocabulary of signs** (aka signary), indexed by gloss-IDs, where each sign will contain: the MoCap data and video of non-inflected signs executed in the same settings as for the sentences, syntactic information of the sign, such as

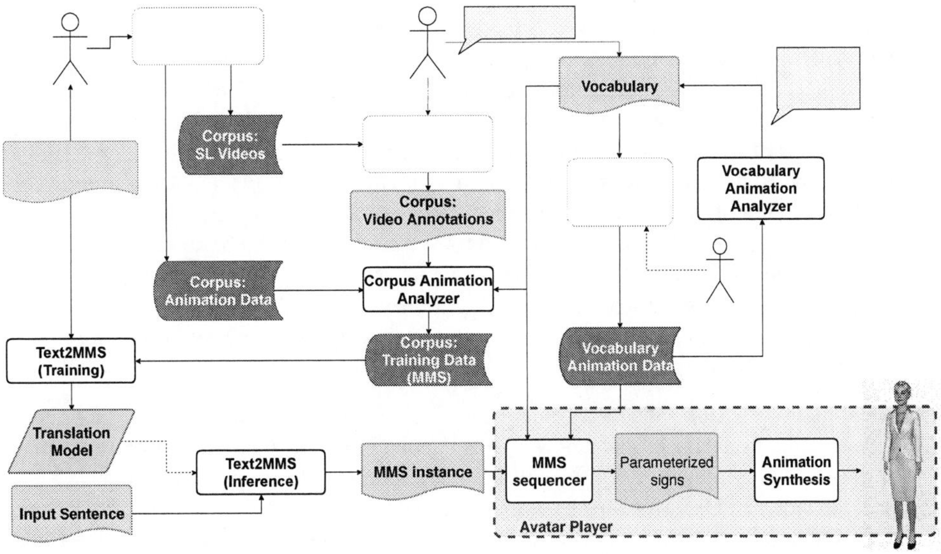

Figure 1: Overview of the off-line training (top) and real-time translation (bottom) pipelines.

symmetry, number of hands, use of mouthing, body contacts, and finally the references to all the possible semantic meanings in WordNet [9].

Third, the annotation process will follow an innovative "boolean-based" simplified annotation scheme, where annotators on each tier must check a flag *only if* the execution of a sign in the sentence shows *meaningful differences* with respect to its lexicalized form in the vocabulary. Here, by "meaningful", we mean deliberate inflections (such as sign relocation, eyebrows movement, body shifts, head movement, facial expressions, and the like) of the sign in order to convey additional meaning. The extraction of the exact values of those differences, i.e., the magnitude of the inflection parameters, is delegated to a procedural analysis of the 3D animation data. Such a simplified annotation strategy is supposedly faster than existing schemes, where annotators must select values from closed lists or insert free text.

Fourth, we are employing a MoCap system that combines different data streams together, like real-time streamed point clouds and multiple (depth) cameras. These different data sources are then combined and processed inclusively to create a matching animation.

2 System Overview

Figure 1 shows a diagram of the offline and realtime phases of the proposed architecture.

Motion Capture The corpus creation starts from a set of written sentences that are translated into sign language and recorded with both a video camera and a full-body motion capture system (fingers, hands, arms, torso, head, and face). The recording is performed simultaneously, so to have a perfect match between the video and the animation data recording.

Annotation The video material will be annotated using the annotation tool NOVA [1]. Here, the data is stored in a collaborative annotation database, so that the annotation work can be divided among several users. In addition, machine learning methods can be integrated into

NOVA with the goal of generating annotations in part automatically. We will train different neural networks for this purpose in an attempt to reduce the workload of the annotators.

The main tier of the annotation scheme is the **gloss** tier, which consist of the time segmentation to identify the beginning and end of a sign. Within each time slot, the annotator inserts the gloss-ID of the vocabulary. Two additional tiers annotate if the dominant or non-dominant hand are performing another sign, holding the previous one, or placing a classifier in the signing space. Each of the remaining tiers must be checked with a boolean *true* only if *meaningful differences* with the vocabulary are noticed for the movement of the **manual elements** (configuration, location, orientation), **non-manuals** (torso, shoulders, head, mouth/mouthings, cheecks, eyes, eyebrows, facial expression); flagging a difference will trigger the automatic computation of *inflection parameters*. Finally, explicit **grammar roles** (wh-question, yes/no question, negation) are also annotated.

Vocabulary creation The vocabulary is created interactively during the annotation of the segmentation tiers. Each time a new sign is encountered, the annotator will insert a new entry in the vocabulary. Each new sign will be then motion-captured in its non-inflected form and both the video and the MoCap data associated to the vocabulary entry. Each entry is completed with annotations about the number of used hands, if it is relocatable in space, if there is contact with other body parts or between hands, mouthing or mouth gestures, and references to all appropriate WordNet synsets [9].

Animation data analysis The Corpus Animation Analyzer computes the inflection parameters that transform signs from their non-inflected form into the way they appear in the sentences. The implementation is based on trajectories transformation (e.g., [2]) and mesh registration (see [17] for a survey). As a result, inflection parameters will take the form of 4D matrices for non-rigid 3D transformations or vectors for corrective blendshape weighting. The output of the analysis–the MMS (multi-modal signstream)–consists of the annotated sentences augmented with the sign inflection parameters.

Automatic translation The Text2MMS is a machine learning module in charge of the conversion between written text and the MMS abstraction. For the task, we will train a neural network that takes sequences of words as input and outputs the most probable class for each element in the vocabulary. Inflection parameters will be predicted as continuous real numbers. Given that machine learning heavily depends on the amount of data used for training, and the corpus might not achieve consistent sizes in the short term, we will adopt both transfer learning and data augmentation techniques. In the first case, we will use pre-trained language models that will be fine-tuned to perform our task [3]. In the second case, we will generate synthetic data using the relations in WordNet, word classes, and our vocabulary joined with unsupervised methods when possible [19, 4].

Avatar creation For the character creation, a state-of-the-art 3D computer graphic program (e.g., Autodesk 3ds Max) will be used. For the development of the photorealistic avatar a 3D photo-scan system for generating high level realistic face textures will be build up. To avoid errors potentially introduced while retargeting between the MoCap data and the avatar's skeleton, the avatar is tuned according to body measurements on the actor. As suggested in previous research [8], we will apply high contrast between skin, clothes and background color, and will provide careful lighting with shadows for a 3D effect.

Avatar animation The avatar animation consists of parsing MMS sequences, and play back the resulting animation data. For the animation synthesis, we use the cloud-based Charamel software VuppetMaster [18], which supports a 3D real-time rendering engine based on WebGL standard, thus making it possible to run the avatar on all known devices (including browsers).

The animation of hands and torso will be driven by inverse kinematic chains. Fifty-one facial action units can be used for creating expressive facial animations, which is fundamental for the comprehension of sign language [7].

User Evaluation With pursuing a human-centered approach within the project, ensuring a focus on the needs of those who are supposed to use and understand the avatar, is essential. Evaluations by and exchange with the target group is thus integrated into the entire process—starting with elaborate measures of user research in early phases (requirements analysis such as personas, scenarios, and user stories) that form the foundation for formative and summative evaluations conducted within usability labs later on. In this way, we want to achieve not only a high acceptance and quality of the avatar, but also strengthen the acceptance and support within the SL-community towards our project's approach.

Ensuring the sign language quality An essential part of project is the continuous checking of the sign language quality of the avatar to be developed. This is achieved through the collaboration with a team of sign language experts and professional interpreters who supervise the annotation process and ensure a high quality standard of the avatar with regard to the representation of sign language. In this way, representatives of the future user group work actively within the realization of the avatar and influence the development according to their requirements.

3 Current Status and Future Work

At the moment of writing, the project completed its initial investigation stage and it is at the beginning of its development stage. The corpus structure has been finalized. The MoCap environment has been tested, finalized, and was used to capture the first sentences of the corpus. The annotation tool has been configured and sign language experts are using it. Scripts to automatize the processing of the corpus (e.g., extraction of facial animation data from videos, consistency check) are under development. The avatar animation engine can playback motion captured sentences and non-inflected signs with body and hands. As soon as facial animation is supported, the avatar will undergo the first user evaluation. Tools for the analysis of the animation data (such as trajectory transformation and mesh registration) are under investigation.

As a first goal, the system shall enable translations for public services, which is characterized by a formal communication register. In the future, the system will be extended to be applied in different contexts, where more complex sign language features, such as iconicity, pose higher challenges for the whole translation pipeline.

References

[1] Tobias Baur, Alexander Heimerl, Florian Lingenfelser, Johannes Wagner, Michel F. Valstar, Björn Schuller, and Elisabeth André. eXplainable cooperative machine learning with NOVA. *KI - Künstliche Intelligenz*, January 2020.

[2] Arie Croitoru, Peggy Agouris, and Anthony Stefanidis. 3D trajectory matching by pose normalization. In *Proceedings of the 2005 international workshop on Geographic information systems - GIS '05*, page 153, Bremen, Germany, 2005. ACM Press.

[3] Jacob Devlin, Ming-Wei Chang, Kenton Lee, and Kristina Toutanova. BERT: Pre-training of deep bidirectional transformers for language understanding. In *Proceedings of the 2019 Conference of the North American Chapter of the Association for Computational Linguistics: Human Language Technologies, Volume 1 (Long and Short Papers)*, pages 4171–4186, Minneapolis, Minnesota, June 2019. Association for Computational Linguistics.

[4] Bosheng Ding, Linlin Liu, Lidong Bing, Canasai Kruengkrai, Thien Hai Nguyen, Shafiq R. Joty, Luo Si, and Chunyan Miao. Daga: Data augmentation with a generation approach for low-resource tagging tasks. *CoRR*, abs/2011.01549, 2020.

[5] Thomas Hanke. HamNoSys-representing sign language data in language resources and language processing contexts. In *LREC*, volume 4, pages 1–6, 2004.

[6] Trevor Johnston. From archive to corpus: Transcription and annotation in the creation of signed language corpora. *International Journal of Corpus Linguistics*, 15(1):106–131, April 2010.

[7] Michael Kipp, Alexis Heloir, and Quan Nguyen. Sign language avatars: Animation and comprehensibility. In *International Workshop on Intelligent Virtual Agents*, pages 113–126. Springer, 2011.

[8] Michael Kipp, Quan Nguyen, Alexis Heloir, and Silke Matthes. Assessing the deaf user perspective on sign language avatars. In *The proceedings of the 13th international ACM SIGACCESS conference on Computers and accessibility*, pages 107–114, 2011.

[9] George A. Miller. WordNet: a lexical database for English. *Communications of the ACM*, 38(11):39–41, November 1995.

[10] Lucie Naert, Caroline Larboulette, and Sylvie Gibet. A survey on the animation of signing avatars: From sign representation to utterance synthesis. *Computers & Graphics*, 92:76–98, November 2020.

[11] AVASAG project web page. https://avasag.de, 2021.

[12] EASIER project web page. https://www.project-easier.eu, 2021.

[13] SignON project web page. https://signon-project.eu, 2021.

[14] Ben Saunders, Necati Cihan Camgöz, and Richard Bowden. Continuous 3d multi-channel sign language production via progressive transformers and mixture density networks. *Int. J. Comput. Vis.*, 129(7):2113–2135, 2021.

[15] Dimitar Shterionov, Vincent Vandeghinste, Horacio Saggion, Josep Blat, Mathieu De Coster, Joni Dambre, Henk Van den Heuvel, Irene Murtagh, Lorraine Leeson, and Ineke Schuurman. The signon project: a sign language translation framework. In *Proceedings of the 31st Meeting of Computational Linguistics in The Netherlands (CLIN 31)*, July 2021.

[16] William Stokoe. *Sign language structure: An outline of the visual communication systems of the American deaf.* Univ. of Buffalo, Buffalo, NY, 1960.

[17] Oliver van Kaick, Hao Zhang, Ghassan Hamarneh, and Daniel Cohen-Or. A Survey on Shape Correspondence. *Computer Graphics Forum*, 30(6):1681–1707, September 2011.

[18] VuppetMaster web page. https://vuppetmaster.de, 2021.

[19] Jason Wei and Kai Zou. EDA: Easy data augmentation techniques for boosting performance on text classification tasks. In *Proceedings of the 2019 Conference on Empirical Methods in Natural Language Processing and the 9th International Joint Conference on Natural Language Processing (EMNLP-IJCNLP)*, pages 6382–6388, Hong Kong, China, November 2019. Association for Computational Linguistics.

Using Computer Vision to Analyze Non-manual Marking of Questions in KRSL

Anna Kuznetsova kuzannagood@gmail.com
School of Linguistics, NRU HSE, Moscow, Russia

Alfarabi Imashev alfarabi.imashev@nu.edu.kz
Department of Robotics and Mechatronics, School of Engineering and Digital Sciences, Nazarbayev University, Nur-Sultan, Kazakhstan

Medet Mukushev mmukushev@nu.edu.kz
Department of Robotics and Mechatronics, School of Engineering and Digital Sciences, Nazarbayev University, Nur-Sultan, Kazakhstan

Anara Sandygulova anara.sandygulova@nu.edu.kz
Department of Robotics and Mechatronics, School of Engineering and Digital Sciences, Nazarbayev University, Nur-Sultan, Kazakhstan

Vadim Kimmelman vadim.kimmelman@uib.no
Department of Linguistic, Literary and Aesthetic Studies, University of Bergen

Abstract

This paper presents a study that compares non-manual markers of polar and wh-questions to statements in Kazakh-Russian Sign Language (KRSL) in a dataset collected for NLP tasks. The primary focus of the study is to demonstrate the utility of computer vision solutions for the linguistic analysis of non-manuals in sign languages, although additional corrections are required to account for biases in the output. To this end, we analyzed recordings of 10 triplets of sentences produced by 9 native signers using both manual annotation and computer vision solutions (such as OpenFace). We utilize and improve the computer vision solution, and briefly describe the results of the linguistic analysis.

1 Introduction

Non-manual marking, that is, linguistically significant use of the body, head, facial features, and eye gaze, is a prominent feature of sign languages (Pfau and Quer, 2010). For instance, in most sign languages, polar questions are accompanied with raised eyebrows, and some type of head movement (Cecchetto, 2012). While non-manual markers in many sign languages have been previously studied, many other sign languages have not been analyzed before, including Kazakh-Russian Sign Language (KRSL), which we discuss in this study.

Current developments in computer vision provide an opportunity for a large-scale quantitative research on non-manual markers. In this study, we evaluate whether computer vision solutions can be utilized for the analysis of non-manual marking present in sign language video recordings. The objective of this work is to compare non-manual markers in statements and questions in KRSL, and to test a computer vision solution against manual annotations.

2 Background

2.1 Non-manual markers in sign languages

Sign languages employ not only hands, but also the body, the head, and the face in order to express linguistic information. Non-manual markers have been analysed for many sign languages (see Pfau and Quer (2010) for overviews). These markers function on different linguistic levels: phonological, morphological, syntactic, and prosodic.

Question marking in particular has been studied for many sign languages (Cecchetto, 2012). Polar (yes/no) questions seem to be almost universally marked by eyebrow raise on the whole sentence, while content questions (wh-questions) are more varied: some sign languages use eyebrow raise, some use eyebrow lowering, and some a combination of both (Zeshan, 2004). In addition, some type of head movement is reported as a marker for many languages, including backward head tilt (chin moving upwards) and forward head tilt (chin moving downward/forward).[1] The non-manual markers vary in scope: they can align with different constituents in the sentence. Furthermore, recent corpus-based research shows a high degree of variability of non-manual marking of questions, contrary to previous claims of the obligatory nature of such markers (Hodge et al., 2019).

Because of both typological and language-internal variation in non-manual marking of questions in sign languages, it is clearly necessary to conduct more empirical studies of such marking in languages that have not been described yet. In addition, applying novel computer vision techniques can facilitate reliable quantitative analysis and enable quantitative cross-linguistic comparison in future.

2.2 Quantitative approaches to non-manual marking

While there exist quantitative studies of non-manuals in various sign languages, some also based on naturalistic corpus data (Coerts, 1992; Puupponen et al., 2015; Hodge et al., 2019), until very recently quantitative approaches were limited by the data sets and the available techniques of analysing non-manuals. Many projects in the past employed manual annotation of non-manual markers, which is both extremely time-consuming and potentially unreliable (Puupponen et al., 2015). Moreover, manual annotation rarely provides the amplitude of non-manuals – in most cases annotation only states the existence of the marker. A more reliable alternative has been to use motion tracking to record precise quantitative data (Puupponen et al., 2015) e.g. on head movement. However, using a motion tracking set up is costly, and the signers have to wear trackers, which make the data recorded this way very far from naturalistic.

Currently two developments have made a large-scale quantitative studies of non-manual marking possible. First, large naturalistic corpora have been created for several sign languages (Crasborn et al., 2008; Konrad et al., 2020). Second, computer vision techniques now allow tracking of the body and facial features in video recordings without any trackers (see references in Section 4). The field of sign language translation has already benefited from these and other factors (see (Camgoz et al., 2018) for a brief overview), however most models only consider hand signs (Zimmermann and Brox, 2017) and other models do not interpret the video features at all (Li et al., 2020). Therefore we are just starting a discussion on the applicability of machine learning methods to non-manual feature extraction in sign languages. In this study, we test the applicability of computer vision to studying question marking using a controlled data set of statements and questions in Kazakh-Russian Sign Language.

[1] Other markers relevant for question marking include eye aperture, eye gaze direction, and body movements, but we do not consider them in this study (Cecchetto, 2012).

2.3 Kazakh-Russian Sign Language (KRSL)

KRSL is the language used primarily by the deaf and hard-of-hearing people in Kazakhstan. We use the term KRSL to acknowledge the fact that this language is closely related to Russian Sign Language due to the common history in the times of the Soviet Union. While no formal comparison between the two languages has been conducted, anecdotally the two languages are fully mutually intelligible, and not considered as separate languages by the deaf signers. Note, however, that KRSL signs can be accompanied by Kazakh mouthings.

Question marking in KRSL has not been described before. Based on the typological research cited above, we had a strong expectation that eyebrow position and head movement would be used to mark questions in KRSL, and that polar questions would be marked with raised eyebrows; we did not have a clear expectation about the eyebrow position in wh-questions.

3 Methodology

3.1 Participants and data collection

We collected video recordings from 9 native signers of KRSL: five deaf signers, and four interpreters, who are hearing children of deaf adults (CODAs). The data set analysed here is a part of a larger data set collected for a different project on automatic sign language recognition.[2]

We created a list of 10 simple sentences consisting of a subject and an intransitive verb. Each of the sentences was collected in three forms: statement (1a), polar question (1b), and wh-question (1c). The former two types of sentences thus contained two signs, and the latter type contained three signs due to the presence of a wh-sign.

1. (a) GIRL FALL 'A girl fell.' (b) GIRL FALL? 'Did the girl fall?' (c) WHERE GIRL FALL? 'Where did the girl fall?'

The stimuli were presented in written Russian to the hearing signers, and as video recordings in KRSL to the deaf signers. We did not use filler sentences, nor concealed from the signers that we were interested in question marking in KRSL. Our aim was thus not to create a maximally naturalistic data set, but a controlled data set with uniform structures produced by several signers for experimenting with computational approaches. No explicit instructions were given about the non-manuals, so we expected the signers to produce the markers natural to them.

Given that the data set was created for the purposes of automatic sign language recognition, and not for research on the grammar of KRSL, and due to the relatively small pool of signers which also includes hearing CODAs, the current study can only be considered describing non-manual marking of questions in this specific data set, and not in KRSL in natural settings. However, we believe that this is a first step towards a more broader research. Furthermore, the size of the data set is quite small, so further testing of the approach with larger data sets will be required in future.

3.2 Manual annotation

As the first step in research, we watched all the videos in order to get a qualitative picture of the non-manual patterns. For polar questions, it turned out that the main non-manual markers were eyebrow raise on the whole sentence and two consecutive forward head tilts on the subject and verb (2). For wh-questions, it was eyebrow raise on the whole sentence or only on the wh-sign and a backward head tilt on the whole sentence or the wh-sign (3-4). It was also noticeable that, in wh-questions, the signers had less consistency in their marking.

[2]All the data used in this study as described below is available at `https://github.com/kuzanna2016/non-manuals-2020`.

2. 

br_raise

head_forward head_forward

DOG EAT

'Is the dog eating?'

3. 

br_raise

chin_up

WHERE CHILD DANCE

'Where the child is dancing?'

4. 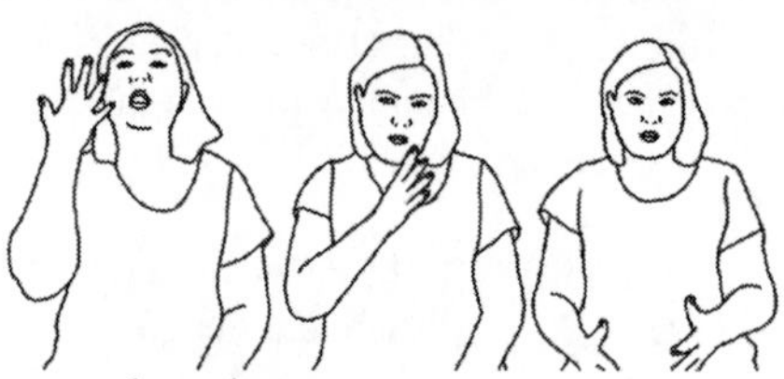

br_raise

chin_up

WHEN MOM TIRED

'When was mom tired?'

With these observations, it was decided that we need to manually annotate eyebrow movement and head tilts. Besides that, the manual signs were annotated to determine the boundaries of the constituents, and the syntactic roles of the constituents (subject, verb, wh-word) were annotated. The annotations were made by the first author, according to the Corpus NGT Annotation Conventions (Crasborn et al., 2015) using the ELAN software (ELAN, 2020).

In order to explore reliability of manual annotation, 20% of randomly selected videos (54 videos) were independently annotated by the last author specifically for eyebrow movement (as later in the paper we assess computer vision measurements of this specific non-manual against manual annotations). Inter-rater agreement was calculated in two different ways: using agreement in category assignment and using the percentage of overlap between the annotations to take duration into account. We found moderate raw agreement for eyebrow movement detection (67%), and even lower agreement in overlap between annotations (57%).

This testing of the reliability of manual annotations is a showcase of the difficulty and subjectivity of this procedure. It is clear that automation of annotation is a necessity. At the same time, the computer vision tools discussed below make it potentially possible to study these subtle phonetic properties of non-manuals.

In some of the videos, the signers produced signs other than the subject, object, and the verb (such as a past tense marker), and in a few videos the subject sign was missing. We removed such videos from further quantitative analysis. Having done that, we had 259 videos in total (88 statements, 82 polar questions, 89 wh-questions).

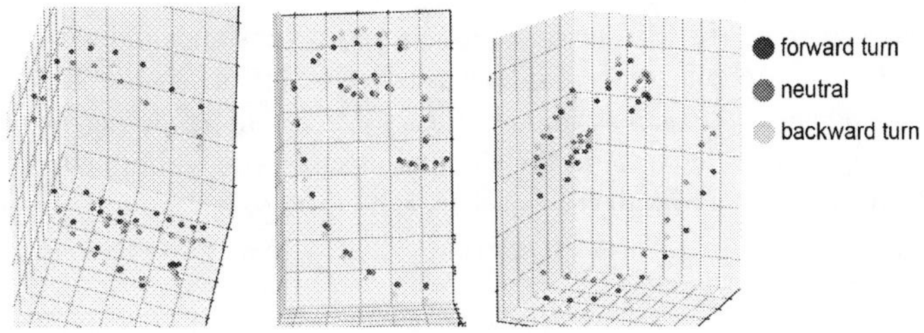

Figure 1: The behaviour of keypoints with different head turns on the test video.

4 Applying computer vision

The field of computer vision is actively developing thanks to the advancements in deep learning. Achievements in this area allow computers to process a large amount of visual information, such as pictures, photos or videos. One of the tasks of computer vision is landmark detection. It can be described as an object recognition task with localization: the algorithm needs not only to detect an object on the image, but also to estimate the position of this object. We planned to use face and head landmarks recognition tools to estimate the eyebrow and head movement.

OpenFace is a toolkit for facial landmark detection, head pose estimation, facial action unit recognition and other facial behaviour analysis (Baltrušaitis et al., 2018, 2013; Zadeh et al., 2017). OpenFace is able to estimate 3D landmarks position from 2D points using Point Distribution Model, which parametrizes the shape of a face using a limited set of parameters, such as scaling, rotation, translation and individual deformations of the face. We used OpenFace 2.2.0 FeatureExtraction model for getting face landmarks position in 3D and head pose estimation for every frame. Face landmarks and head coordinates were in x,y,z-coordinates in mm, and the head rotation angle was in radians with the camera being the origin. The model also provided us with a confidence score for each frame. By outputting head rotation, OpenFace directly provides a measure of forward/backward head tilt that we are interested in for the analysis. However, the estimation of eyebrow position from OpenFace output is less straightforward.

When we visually investigated the OpenFace output, we noticed that the results conflicted with our initial observations. We expected polar questions to have the largest eyebrow raise but OpenFace output was even smaller than in statements. Furthermore, we saw correlation between rotation angle and eyebrow distance, meaning that, probably, OpenFace predictions are prone to bias by the head rotation.

To demonstrate this bias, we plotted 3 frames from our test video of the forward to backward head tilt without eyebrow movement. We rotated the face keypoints in the reverse angle of the computed head rotation and centred them on the bridge of the nose keypoint number 27. From Figure 1, we can see that the face points, especially eyebrow points, are bending. Hence, the 3D model that OpenFace deduces is likely to be distorted in the presence of head movement. We therefore had to attempt to eliminate such distortions.

General 3D reconstruction from a single camera is a really challenging problem and it is outside of our area of competence, therefore we were not able to modify the OpenFace model itself. Moreover, we do not have the specifically annotated data with facial landmarks to retrain the model. That is why we will deal with the computed output instead of the model.

To deal with the bias we created a machine learning model that would predict the eyebrows distance depending on the head rotation when the eyebrows were not raised or lowered, i.e. the default eyebrow distance with the influence of tilting. We trained linear regression with L2 regularization and alpha 0.001 from *sklearn* library for Python (Pedregosa et al., 2018) on statements that contained no eyebrow raises: 63 sentences (4414 frames). The target of the model was the distance from the eyebrow points (18, 23 - inner, 20, 25 - outer) to the eye line -

a line between points 36, 45. The mean inner eyebrow distance in the subset was 29.7 and the outer was 27.1. Our choice of the model was based on the observation that the distortion seems to be linear and consistent across signers – Pearson correlation coefficient between vertical head angle and the eyebrow distance to the eye line in sentences with no eyebrow raise is -0.42 for the inner distance and -0.48 for the outer distance. Moreover, the training data set is small and thus a simple model should be sufficient.

Model №	Features	inner MSE	outer MSE
1	cos, sin, tan of vertical and horizontal head angles; nose length (distance between points 27 and 30)	4	
2	+ signer IDs and sentence IDs	1.61	1.54
3	+ the vertical eye distances	1.45	1.36

Table 1: Models' features description and the results

The features of the models that we used are shown in Table 1. We did not use the angle of rotation in the z-axis (from the ears to the shoulders) because it worsened the result for such turns. We did not use pure radians for rotation, because they shifted the model to some incomprehensible extremes.[3] In all our experiments we used 5-split random permutation cross-validation with test proportion of 25% (731 frames) to make sure the model does not overfit.

The first model performed with an MSE of about 4 for each eyebrow distance. However we wanted a better result. We added meta information as one-hot encoded vectors and it significantly increased the quality on the cross-validation. We believe that this allowed the model to learn the individual mean eyebrow height for each signer. We also noticed that blinking affected the distance estimation, so we added eye aperture features, which slightly reduced the error.[4]

After training the final model on statements, the eyebrow distance was predicted for all sentences, and then subtracted from the distance computed on OpenFace output directly. Thus, we subtracted the changes in distance caused by the tilts from the distance based on the output to get the unbiased distance measurement.

To check that this approach produced reasonable results, we looked manually at 35 sentences and compared the predictions with the annotations. In general, the output of the model agreed with our annotations. Furthermore, the correlation between the vertical head tilt and the new eyebrow distance is lower than on the original distance (-0.27 for inner, -0.25 for outer). Having demonstrated that this method of adjusting the eyebrow distance for head movement works well, we conducted the subsequent analysis using it.

5 Statistical analysis

One of the main advantages of applying computer vision to analysis of non-manuals in sign languages is that it opens the possibility of consequent advanced statistical analysis, instead of relying on qualitative observations. Thus, we use the current data set to showcase a possible statistical analysis of the output of the proposed computer vision approach.

We analyzed the data in R (version 3.6.3) using R Studio (version 1.0.143) (R Core Team, 2020; RStudio Team, 2020). For this study, we averaged the eyebrows distance in each video in the parts of sentence areas for inner eyebrows points (20,23) and for outer eyebrows points

[3] We also deleted the frames that had low OpenFace confidence (<0.8) - 103 frames from 12 videos in total.

[4] It was our decision to select specific data set features to increase the accuracy of the model. Thus the current model would not generalize to other data sets and we encourage other researchers to retrain it on their data or use the first model without the meta features.

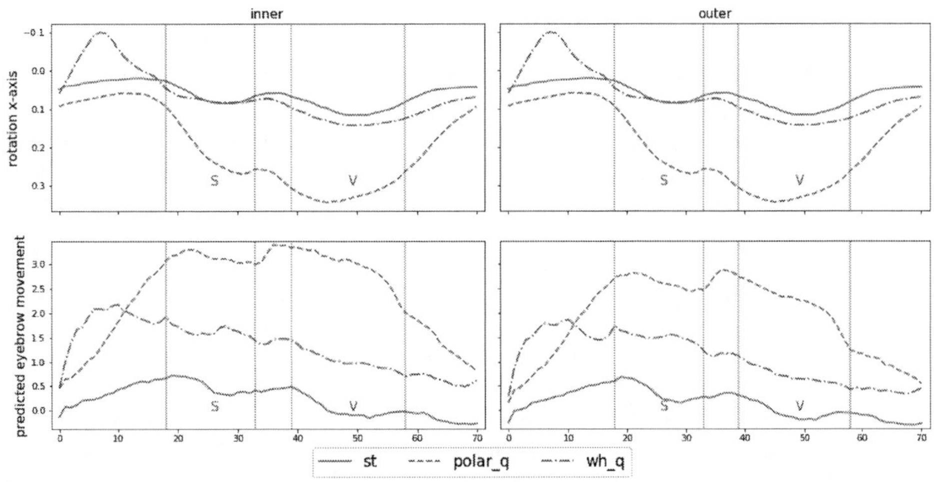

Figure 2: Mean head rotation angle and predicted difference in eyebrow movement for three sentence types. Vertical lines define the beginning and ending of the part of sentence tag (S - subject, V - verb). Rotation graphs are reversed in y-axis for interpretation (lower angle - backward head tilt, higher angle - forward head tilt).

(18,25) (averaging the left and right eyebrow distance). Thus, we had four eyebrow measurements for all the sentences (inner and outer mean distance for the subject and inner and outer mean distance for the verb) and separately we had six eyebrow measurements for the wh-questions (inner and outer mean distance for the wh-sign, subject, and verb). Besides, we calculated the mean head rotation angle on the x-axis (vertical tilts) again for two signs for all the sentences and for three signs for the wh-questions.

A mixed-effects multivariate linear regression model was picked for the analysis (Baayen et al., 2008; Bates et al., 2014). We made 9 models with the outcome variables of internal and external eyebrow distances and head tilt angle on the subjects, verbs, and wh-questions.

The fixed predictor variables for the first 6 models were sentence type (categorical, three levels: statement, polar question, wh-question), group (categorical, deaf vs. hearing), and all the interactions between the two predictors. For the last three models, the fixed predictor variables were part of sentence (categorical, three levels: wh-word, subject, verb), group (categorical, deaf vs. hearing), and all the interactions between the two predictors. We used orthogonal coding of contrasts for the predictors with three levels. Finally, for all models, the random variables were participant (with a random slope for sentence type or part of sentence), and sentence (with a random slope for group).

For the models, we used the *lme4* package (Chung et al., 2015) with the help of the *blme* package to achieve convergence with a small number of levels for the random effects (Chung et al., 2013). The significance of the contribution of the factors was computed with the *ANOVA* function from the *car* package (Fox and Weisberg, 2019).

6 Results

Firstly, we examined the results visually. From Figure 2, we can see that: polar questions have tilting forward on the subject and verb and eyebrows raise on the whole question, while wh-questions have tilting backwards on the wh-word and eyebrows raise in the beginning on the wh-word, which is slowly declining to the end of the sentence. In all the statistical analyses below, the effect of group and interactions between the group and the other effects were never significant, so we do not discuss them further.

6.1 Eyebrow movement

We find that sentence type significantly influences both internal and external eyebrows distance on the subject and the verb (ANOVA χ^2 show significance at p<0.001 for all the comparisons).

For internal eyebrow points, the eyebrows distance is bigger for wh-questions than statements on the subject by estimated 1 mm (*se* = 0.64, *t* = 1.57), and on the verb by 0.87 mm (*se* = 0.5, *t* = 1.76). The average between statement and wh-question is lower than polar questions by 2.05 mm (*se* = 0.46, *t* = 4.48) on the subject and 2.34 mm (*se* = 0.55, *t* = 4.23) on the verb.

For external eyebrow points, the eyebrows distance is bigger for wh-questions than statements on the subject by estimated 1 mm (*se* = 0.65, *t* = 1.5), and on the verb by estimated 0.63 mm (*se* = 0.5, *t* = 1.27). The average between statement and wh-question is less than polar questions by estimated 1.66 mm (*se* = 0.43, *t* = 3.89) on the subject and 1.77 mm (s*se* = 0.6, *t* = 2.91) on the verb. The difference in distance is lower for the external eyebrows than for the internal eyebrows (but note that we did not quantitatively compare these differences).

In wh-questions, we find that the part of the sentence influences the eyebrow distance (ANOVA χ^2 for internal = 7.362, df = 2, p<0.05, for external = 6.824, df = 2, p <0.05).

Internal eyebrows distance on the subject is bigger than on the verb by 0.5 mm (*se* = 0.5, *t* = 1.09). The average between internal eyebrows distance on subject and verb is less than on the wh-word by 0.73 mm (*se* = 0.38, *t* = 1.9). External eyebrows distance on the subject is bigger than on the verb by 0.68 mm (*se* = 0.47, *t* = 1.43). The average between external eyebrows distance on subject and verb is less than on the wh-word by 0.59 mm (*se* = 0.4, *t* = 1.43).

To sum up, we confirmed our initial hypothesis that polar questions and wh-questions are marked with eyebrow raise both internal and external. Besides, we find indications that the contour of the raise is different in these sentence types, even though we have not tested the significance of these differences as the estimates come from different models. The eyebrow raise in polar questions is higher on the verb than on the subject, whereas in wh-questions it is higher on the subject than on the verb. Also, the raise itself is smaller in wh-questions.

Moreover, we analyzed the eyebrow raise in wh-questions separately and found out that eyebrows raise starts at the wh-word and then gradually decreases.

6.2 Head movement

As we stated before, vertical head tilts are measured in radian angles on the x-axis. A positive angle means forward tilt, whereas a negative angle means head tilt backwards.

We find that sentence type influences the head rotation angle on the subject and the verb (ANOVA χ^2 for subject 8.819, df = 2, p <0.05, for verb 10.462, df = 2, p <0.01). The head rotation angle is bigger for wh-questions than statements on the subject by estimated 0.006 radians (*se* = 0.029, *t* = 0.22), and on the verb by estimated 0.03 radians (*se* = 0.02, *t* = 1.4). The average between statement and wh-question is lower than polar questions by estimated 0.13 radians (*se* = 0.046, *t* = 2.9) on the subject and 0.2 radians (*se* = 0.06, *t* = 3.1) on the verb.

In wh-questions, we find that the part of the sentence significantly influences the head rotation angle (ANOVA χ^2 = 39.887, df = 2, p <0.001). Rotation angle on the subject is less by estimated 0.06 radians (*se* = 0.02, *t* =-2.6) than on the verb. Rotation angle is less on the wh-word than on the average between subject and verb by 0.16 radians (*se* = 0.04, *t* = -4.19).

To conclude, as we saw in Figure 2, polar questions differ from wh-questions and statements regarding head tilting forward on the subject and verb. Meanwhile, the difference between wh-questions and statements is not significant (0.006 radians and 0.032 radians on subject and verb respectively). However, when examining wh-questions separately, we confirmed that the wh-word is marked with a head tilt backwards (-0.16 radians) in contrast to the other part of the sentence, and this difference is significant.

7 Discussion

7.1 Non-manual question marking in the KRSL dataset

Our study provides a first description of non-manual question marking in KRSL by analyzing a dataset created for NLP purposes. As discussed above, it is inadvisable to generalize our findings to naturalistic use of KRSL.

Both manual annotations and the quantitative analysis demonstrate that polar questions in the dataset are marked by forward head tilt on the subject and the verb, and eyebrow raise on the whole sentence; wh-questions are marked by backward head tilt on the wh-sign, and by eyebrow raise on the wh-sign that can also spread to the whole sentence, but the raise is smaller than in polar questions. This dataset thus neatly fits the most common typological pattern for non-manual marking of questions in sign languages (Cecchetto, 2012).

7.2 Applicability of computer vision

This study demonstrates that it is possible to apply modern computer vision tools to analyze non-manual markers in sign languages quantitatively.

OpenFace (Baltrušaitis et al., 2018, 2013; Zadeh et al., 2017) provides a solution to the problem of using 2D video recordings for analysis by reconstructing a 3D model of the face from the 2D representation. However, our experiments show that the reconstructed 3D model is still sensitive to distortions due to some types of movement (specifically, due to forward and backward head tilts). We developed a solution for this problem by applying machine learning in order to teach a new model to account for the bias introduced by the head tilts.

Based on this experience, we can also offer a **practical recommendation** for linguists planning to use OpenFace or similar tools for the analysis of non-manual markers. In case the study involves novel data collection, it would be very useful to record each subject rotating their head in various directions without moving the eyebrows or any other articulators on the face. These recordings can be later use to train a model similar to the one described in this study to correct for distortions due to head tilts. In our data set we fortunately had some recordings that could be used as such a training data set, but it is better to plan for such a data set directly.

8 Conclusions

This paper presents the analysis of non-manual marking of simple polar and wh-questions in KRSL produced by nine native KRSL signers for a dataset for automatic sign language translation. To this end, we firstly annotated the data set manually, and then applied computer vision techniques to automate extraction of non-manual marking from video recordings.

Our findings suggest that polar questions in the KRSL dataset are marked by an eyebrow raise on the whole sentence, and by consecutive forward head tilts on the subject and the verb. In addition, wh-questions are marked by backward head tilts on the wh-sign, and by an eyebrow raise on the wh-sign that can spread over the whole sentence.

Additionally, we demonstrated the utility of computer vision solutions, specifically, OpenFace (Baltrušaitis et al., 2018, 2013; Zadeh et al., 2017) that can be applied to sign language data for the purpose of linguistic analysis of non-manual marking. However, we also discovered that head movement leads to distortion of the facial features even though OpenFace reconstructs a 3D model of the face to account for such movement. We addressed this problem with a machine learning solution.

References

Baayen, H., Davidson, D., and Bates, D. (2008). Mixed-effects modeling with crossed random effects for subjects and items. *Journal of Memory and Language*, 59:390–412.

Baltrušaitis, T., Robinson, P., and Morency, L.-P. (2013). Constrained local neural fields for robust facial landmark detection in the wild. In *2013 IEEE International Conference on Computer Vision Workshops*, pages 354–361.

Baltrušaitis, T., Zadeh, A., Lim, Y. C., and Morency, L.-P. (2018). Openface 2.0: Facial behavior analysis toolkit. In *2018 13th IEEE International Conference on Automatic Face Gesture Recognition (FG 2018)*, pages 59–66.

Bates, D., Mächler, M., Bolker, B., and Walker, S. (2014). Fitting linear mixed-effects models using lme4. *ArXiv e-prints*, arXiv:1406.

Camgoz, N. C., Hadfield, S., Koller, O., Ney, H., and Bowden, R. (2018). Neural sign language translation. In *2018 IEEE/CVF Conference on Computer Vision and Pattern Recognition*, pages 7784–7793.

Cecchetto, C. (2012). Sentence types. In Pfau, R., Steinbach, M., and Woll, B., editors, *Sign language: An international handbook*, pages 292–315. De Gruyter Mouton.

Chung, Y., Gelman, A., Rabe-Hesketh, S., Liu, J., and Dorie, V. (2015). Weakly informative prior for point estimation of covariance matrices in hierarchical models. *Journal of Educational and Behavioral Statistics*, 40:136–157.

Chung, Y., Rabe-Hesketh, S., Dorie, V., Gelman, A., and Liu, J. (2013). A nondegenerate penalized likelihood estimator for variance parameters in multilevel models. *Psychometrika*, 78:685–709.

Coerts, J. (1992). *Nonmanual Grammatical Markers. An Analysis of Interrogatives, Negation and Topicalisation in Sign Language of the Netherlands.* Doctoral dissertation, University of Amsterdam.

Crasborn, O., Bank, R., Zwitserlood, I., van der Kooij, E., Meijer, A., Sáfár, A., and Ormel, E. (2015). *Annotation Conventions for the Corpus NGT, version 3.*

Crasborn, O., Zwitserlood, I., and Ros, J. (2008). Corpus NGT. an open access digital corpus of movies with annotations of Sign Language of the Netherlands.

ELAN (2020). ELAN (Version 5.9) [Computer software]. Nijmegen: Max Planck Institute for Psycholinguistics, The Language Archive.

Fox, J. and Weisberg, S. (2019). *An R Companion to Applied Regression.* Sage, Thousand Oaks CA, third edition.

Hodge, G., Fenlon, J., Schembri, A., Johnston, T., and Cormier, K. (2019). A corpus-based investigation of how deaf signers signal questions during conversation. Poster presented at the 13th Theoretical Issues in Sign Language conference, Universität Hamburg, Germany.

Konrad, R., Hanke, T., Langer, G., Blanck, D., Bleicken, J., Hofmann, I., Jeziorski, O., König, L., König, S., Nishio, R., Regen, A., Salden, U., Wagner, S., Worseck, S., Böse, O., Jahn, E., and Schulder, M. (2020). MY DGS annotated. public corpus of German Sign Language, 3rd release MEINE DGS annotiert. Öffentliches korpus der deutschen gebärdensprache, 3. release.

Li, D., Xu, C., Yu, X., Zhang, K., Swift, B., Suominen, H., and Li, H. (2020). Tspnet: Hierarchical feature learning via temporal semantic pyramid for sign language translation.

Pedregosa, F., Varoquaux, G., Gramfort, A., Michel, V., Thirion, B., Grisel, O., Blondel, M., Müller, A., Nothman, J., Louppe, G., Prettenhofer, P., Weiss, R., Dubourg, V., Vanderplas, J., Passos, A., Cournapeau, D., Brucher, M., Perrot, M., and Édouard Duchesnay (2018). Scikit-learn: Machine learning in python.

Pfau, R. and Quer, J. (2010). Nonmanuals: their prosodic and grammatical roles. In Brentari, D., editor, *Sign Languages*, pages 381–402. Cambridge University Press.

Puupponen, A., Wainio, T., Burger, B., and Jantunen, T. (2015). Head movements in Finnish Sign Language on the basis of Motion Capture data: A study of the form and function of nods, nodding, head thrusts, and head pulls. *Sign Language & Linguistics*, 18(1):41–89.

R Core Team (2020). *R: A Language and Environment for Statistical Computing*. R Foundation for Statistical Computing, Vienna, Austria.

RStudio Team (2020). *RStudio: Integrated Development Environment for R*. RStudio, PBC., Boston, MA.

Zadeh, A., Baltrušaitis, T., and Morency, L.-P. (2017). Convolutional experts constrained local model for facial landmark detection.

Zeshan, U. (2004). Interrogative constructions in signed languages: Crosslinguistic perspectives. *Language*, 80(1):7–39.

Zimmermann, C. and Brox, T. (2017). Learning to estimate 3d hand pose from single RGB images. *CoRR*, abs/1705.01389.

Approaching Sign Language Gloss Translation as a Low-Resource Machine Translation Task

Xuan Zhang xuanzhang@jhu.edu
Kevin Duh kevinduh@cs.jhu.edu
Johns Hopkins University, Baltimore, MD 21218, USA

Abstract

A cascaded Sign Language Translation system first maps sign videos to gloss annotations and then translates glosses into a spoken languages. This work focuses on the second-stage gloss translation component, which is challenging due to the scarcity of publicly available parallel data. We approach gloss translation as a low-resource machine translation task and investigate two popular methods for improving translation quality: hyperparameter search and back-translation. We discuss the potentials and pitfalls of these methods based on experiments on the RWTH-PHOENIX-Weather 2014T dataset.

1 Introduction

More than 70 million deaf people around the world use sign language as their primary language to communicate. In a society dominated by hearing people and spoken languages, there is a risk that deaf people may experience inconvenience and isolation. In countries like India, Iran, and Russia, lack of sign language interpreters hampers access to public services and courts (Kozik, 2019). Automatic Sign Language Translation (SLT) has recently gained increasing attention from researchers and would help remove the communication barriers.

Sign language is not simply a visual form of spoken languages. It has its own linguistic rules, including phonology, morphology, syntax and semantics that are different from other languages (Valli et al., 2011). For example, in American Sign Language, the subject or object might be omitted in certain situations. There is also a process called *Topicalization*, where prominent information is signed first, resulting in an adjustment to the basic SVO word order. Linguists use *glossing* to annotate signs, which can be viewed as a written form of sign language. Glosses can be taken as intermediate representations when translating continuous sign utterances to spoken language sentences.

Previous work on SLT adopts either an end-to-end system that maps sign language videos directly to spoken languages, or a cascaded system, as shown in Figure 1, that first relies on Continuous Sign Language Recognition (CSLR) to produce sign glosses and then passes the glosses into a Neural Machine Translation (NMT) system (Camgoz et al., 2018, 2020; Yin and Read, 2020). Importantly, Camgoz et al. (2018) reports that the cascaded system outperforms the end-to-end system by a large margin (18.13 vs. 9.58 BLEU). In this work, we focus on improving the NMT component of cascaded systems, which attracts much less attentions compared to the CSLR component of cascaded systems (Cui et al., 2017; Huang et al., 2018; Yang et al., 2019; Orbay and Akarun, 2020).

Sign language gloss translation is a challenging problem due to the scarcity of annotated parallel data. The popular continuous SLT dataset, "RWTH-PHOENIX-Weather 2014T" (Camgoz et al., 2018) contains 7,096 gloss-text examples in training set. However, the state-of-the-art

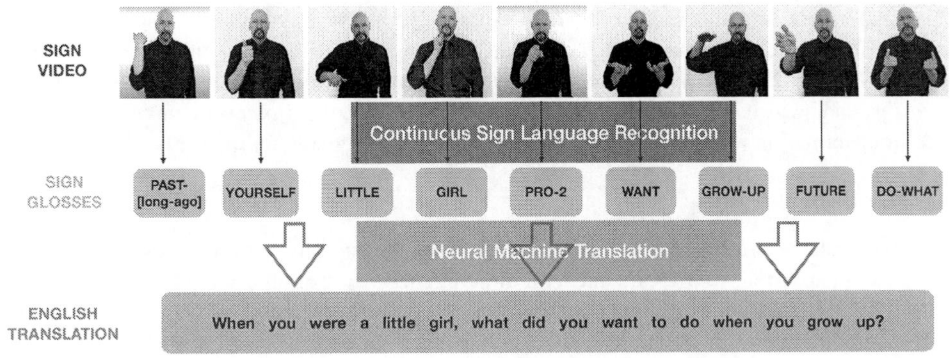

Figure 1: Cascaded sign language translation system[2]- First, CSLR converts sign video to a sequence of sign glosses. Then, NMT converts the sign glosses to text in e.g. English.

NMT systems are known to be extremely data-hungry and usually require millions of training examples to obtain a good translation performance (Koehn and Knowles, 2017). In this paper, we approach gloss to text translation as a low-resource machine translation task and investigate two methods that are widely explored by the machine translation community to alleviate the need of large corpora, namely hyperparameter search and back-translation.

While NMT models, like Transformer (Vaswani et al., 2017) can perform well with default hyperparameter settings on most of the publicly available large corpora, its performance is highly sensitive to hyperparameters under low-resource scenarios (Araabi and Monz, 2020; Duh et al., 2020). The optimal hyperparameter settings for a large corpus might lead to a poor system trained on a small dataset (Zhang and Duh, 2020). In this work, we focus on tuning 4 hyperparameters and find that hyperparameter search is necessary and helpful for gloss translation.

Back-translation (Sennrich et al., 2016a) incorporates monolingual data in NMT which can help in low-resource settings (Hoang et al., 2018; Lample et al., 2018; Feldman and Coto-Solano, 2020). Our experiments show that it has potential on gloss translation when the additional monolingual data are from the same domain as the parallel data.

Overall, we conclude that the low-resource machine translation perspective is promising but should not be taken as the ultimate solution for sign language gloss translation. It may be more promising to first focus on creating larger gloss-text datasets.

2 Related Work

Most of the Sign Language Processing research has focused on Sign Language Recognition (Yin et al., 2016; Wang et al., 2016; Camgöz et al., 2016; Vaezi Joze and Koller, 2019). Recent work started to show an interest in CLSR (Koller et al., 2016; Cui et al., 2017; Huang et al., 2018; Yang et al., 2019; Orbay and Akarun, 2020). However, only a few works move forward to tackle this problem as a SLT task. Camgoz et al. (2018) formalized SLT in the framework of NMT and released the first publicly available SLT dataset, PHOENIX14T. Based on this dataset, Camgoz et al. (2020) and Yin and Read (2020) explored SLT with Transformers and developed both end-to-end and cascaded systems where gloss annotations are used as intermediate representations. Ko et al. (2019) proposed a sign language translation system based on human keypoint estimation and also introduced the KETI dataset, which consists of Korean

[2]Sign videos and glosses are from lifeprint.com.

sign videos and annotations. KETI has only 105 gloss annotations. Also, the sentences in KETI are relatively short as they are related to emergency situations. Othman and Jemni (2012) introduced the ASLG-PC12 dataset, which consists of millions of English sentences and corresponding American sign language glosses. However, the glosses are generated by applying transformation rules on English sentences and are not reliable for the study of SLT.

3 Data and Setup

We evaluate the effectiveness of hyperparameter search on a parallel gloss-text dataset. For back-translation, we experiment with monolingual data from the same domain as the parallel data and data from a different domain respectively. In this section, we will describe the datasets and NMT models in detail. We will also introduce our experimental setup.

3.1 Parallel Data

We use "RWTH-PHOENIX-Weather 2014T" introduced by Camgoz et al. (2018) as our parallel gloss-text dataset. PHOENIX14T collected the weather forecast airings of the German public tv-station PHOENIX. It is a continuous SLT corpus, which contains sign videos, gloss annotations and German translations. The data split for train/dev/test is 7,096/519/642 sentences. The vocabulary size of the training set for glosses and German[3] are 1,066 and 2,887 respectively.

3.2 Monolingual Data

To the best of our knowledge, there is no publicly available large corpus of weather forecast subtitles in German. Since domain mismatch between the monolingual data and the parallel data might hurt the performance of NMT systems (Koehn and Knowles, 2017), we adopt several domain adaption methods to alleviate this problem. We use Moore-Lewis filtering (Moore and Lewis, 2010) to select sentences similar to PHOENIX14T from a German TED Talk corpus (Duh, 2018), which consists of 151,627 sentences.

3.3 NMT Model

Most NMT models in literature follow a encoder-decoder architecture. The conditional probability of generating the target sentence $\boldsymbol{y}$ given the source sentence $\boldsymbol{x}$ is decomposed as:

$$p(\boldsymbol{y} \mid \boldsymbol{x}) = \prod_{j=1}^{J} p(y_j \mid \boldsymbol{y}_{<j}, \boldsymbol{x}, \theta), \tag{1}$$

where θ represents model parameters, y_j is the j-th target word, and $\boldsymbol{y}_{<j}$ is the prefix of words before y_j. The encoder of an NMT model transforms $\boldsymbol{x}$ into a sequence of hidden states, the decoder then generates y_j iteratively based on the hidden states and the history decoding states to form the target sentence $\boldsymbol{y}$. We choose Transformer (Vaswani et al., 2017) as it is the de facto mainstream NMT architecture and has achieved the state-of-the-art performance on many machine translation tasks. Transformer is an encoder-decoder based model with each layer consisting of a multi-head attention mechanism, followed by a feed-forward network.

3.4 Experimental Setup

3.4.1 Data Preprocessing

All datasets are tokenized using the Moses (Koehn et al., 2007) tokenizer. We train the Byte-Pair-Encoding (BPE) segmentation (Sennrich et al., 2016b) models separately for gloss and text. For hyperparameter search experiments (Section 4), we learn BPE models from PHOENIX14T. For back-translation tasks (Section 5), on the German side, we learn BPE models from the

[3]For the rest of this paper, we will refer to sign language gloss as gloss and the spoken German as German.

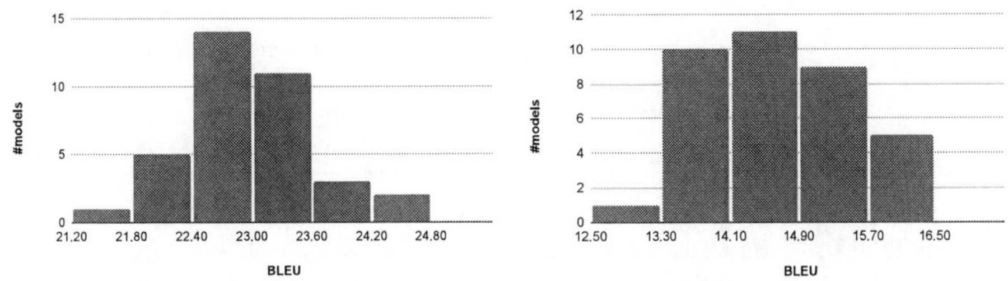

Figure 2: Histograms of BLEU scores showing wide variance in performance with different hyperparameter settings trained on PHOENIX14T gloss-text (left) and text-gloss (right).

concatenation of selected monolingual data and PHOENIX14T data. On the gloss side, we learn BPE models from the concatenation of PHOENIX14T data and the back-translated TED Talk glosses.

3.4.2 NMT Setup

Our NMT models are developed in Sockeye[4] (Hieber et al., 2017). The number of attention heads is set to 8 and the feed-forward layer dimension is set to 1024. We set the dropout probability for source and target embeddings to 0.1. Our models apply Adam (Kingma and Ba, 2014) as the optimizer. The learning rate is multiplied by 0.9 whenever validation perplexity does not surpass the previous best in 8 checkpoints, where checkpoints are encountered for every 1000 updates/batches. And each batch consists of 2048 words. Training stops when the perplexity on the development set has not improved for 32 checkpoints.

All the back-translation experiments in Section 5 adopt the best hyperparameter settings obtained by a hyperparameter search (Section 4). Note that the optimal settings for gloss-text translation is different from text-gloss translation.

4 Hyperparameter Search

Hyperparameter selection is crucial to build a good NMT system. It is especially the case for low-resource scenarios when the default hyperparameter settings are very likely to be ineffective. As reported in Sennrich and Zhang (2019) and Zhang and Duh (2020), the NMT systems developed for low-resource translation tasks disagree a lot with those trained on high-resource corpora on the optimal hyperparameter choices. Furthermore, datasets in different domains and language pairs all differ in their hyperparameter preference. They also show that adjusting hyperparameters can cause BLEU differences of more than 20 in some datasets.

4.1 Important Hyperparameters

In this work, we focus on 4 hyperparameters of Transformer models: the number of BPE merge operations, the number of layers, embedding dimensions and initial learning rate. These hyperparameters are recognized as important hyperparameters by Zhang and Duh (2020), where the importance is computed as the variation in BLEU when changing a specific hyperparameter with values of all the other hyperparameters fixed (Klein and Hutter, 2019).

BPE is a word segmentation approach that combines frequent sequence of characters so that out-of-vocabulary words are handled. It is expected to improve the translation of rare words and has been a standard preprocessing practice in NMT. According to Ding et al. (2019), although 32k and 90k are popular choices in most machine translation literature, they found

[4] `github.com/awslabs/sockeye`

	gloss-text					text-gloss				
	bpe	#layer	#embed	init_lr	**BLEU**	bpe	#layer	#embed	init_lr	**BLEU**
best	1k	4	512	0.00005	**24.38**[5]	1k	4	256	0.0005	**16.43**
worst	2k	1	512	0.0005	**21.73**	1k	1	512	0.0005	**13.04**
random	1k	2	256	0.0002	**23.49**	1k	2	256	0.0002	**15.74**

Table 1: Performance of selected Transformers. BLEU scores are evaluated on the test set of PHOENIX14T. **Best** and **worst** are best and worst systems obtained from hyperparameter search respectively. **Random** randomly picks a hyperparameter setting from our search space.

that the BPE of the best Transformer-based architectures in low-resource setting is somewhere between 0-2k. We thus try 1k and 2k in our experiments.

Architecture design hyperparameters like the number of layers in encoder and decoder and embedding size are important. A big and complex model is more susceptible to overfitting. On the other hand, if the model is too small and simple, it might struggle to capture the meaningful patterns of data and result in underfitting. Our search space includes 1, 2, 4 layers and embedding size of 256 and 512.

The learning rate is another important hyperparameter that scales the gradient in gradient descent training. A small initial learning rate may prolong the training process, whereas a large one may get the model stuck in a sub-optimal solution. It is recommended to start training with a low number (Koehn, 2020). We adjust it among 0.00005, 0.0002 and 0.0005.

We tune hyperparameters for NMT systems on both gloss-text and text-gloss directions. This sums up to 72 systems in total.

4.2 Results

The BLEU scores obtained on our search space are illustrated in Figure 2, where a wide variance is observed. As shown in Table 1, different choices of hyperparameters can increase the BLEU score by as much as 2.65 on gloss-text and 3.39 on text-gloss. Training is not expensive due to the small data size, so running a wide search over hyperparameters is recommended.

5 Back-translation

Back-translation proposed in Sennrich et al. (2016a) has shown its effectiveness in utilizing monolingual data to improve the translation performance. It is particularly used in low-resource scenarios. When it comes to sign language translation, the written text is always abundant, whereas the glosses and parallel examples are expensive to get and are not sufficient to train a robust NMT model. This sets a good stage for back-translation.

The workflow of back-translation is illustrated in Figure 3. In order to train a more robust gloss-text translation model, one first trains a text-gloss model using the PHOENIX14T parallel data (Figure 3, step 1). This model is then employed to translate monolingual German text in the domain of TED Talk to glosses (Figure 3, step 2). This synthetic parallel corpus is then concatenated with the PHOENIX14T data to train the final gloss-text system (Figure 3, step 3).

One problem with our implementation of back-translation is that TED Talk subtitles have different styles compared to PHOENIX14T, which is composed of weather reports, in other words, they are in different domains. Domain mismatch makes the translation task even more challenging, as the synthetic parallel data might introduce noises to hurt the performance. In order to alleviate this issue, we adopt two domain adaptation methods to aid back-translation.

[5]The best BLEU-4 score reported in Camgoz et al. (2020) and Yin and Read (2020) are 24.54 and 24.9, which are comparable to our results.

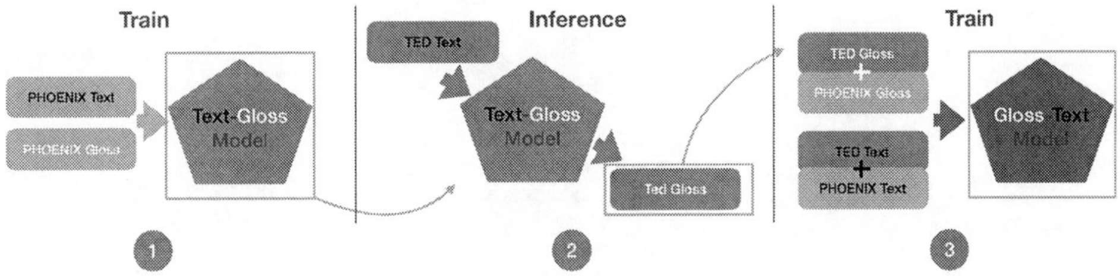

Figure 3: Back-translation workflow. Pink rectangles frame outputs of each step.

5.1 Domain Adaptation Methods

Domain adaptation leverages out-of-domain data to improve the domain-specific translation. In this work, TED Talks are out-of-domain data and PHOENIX14T is the domain in interest or in-domain data. We adopt a language model based data selection method to first select examples from TED Talk corpus that are similar to PHOENIX14T. Next, those monolingual examples are back-translated and form a synthetic parallel corpus. A model is then trained on the concatenation of the synthetic data and the parallel PHOENIX14T data. This is not the end. Finally, we continue training the model with only the PHOENIX14T data. This continued-training process is also called fine-tuning, which is the conventional way for domain adaptation (Luong et al., 2015; Sennrich et al., 2016a; Chu and Wang, 2018; Zhang et al., 2019).

5.1.1 Data Selection

We adopt the data selection method proposed in Moore and Lewis (2010). The main idea is to score the out-of-domain data N using language models trained from the in-domain data I and N and select top n training examples from N by a cut-off threshold on the resulting scores. To be specific, each sentence s in N is assigned a cross-entropy difference score,

$$H_I(s) - H_N(s), \tag{2}$$

where $H_I(s)$ is the per-word cross-entropy of s according to a language model trained on 1000 random samples of PHOENIX14T, and $H_N(s)$ is the per-word cross-entropy of s according to a language model trained on 1000 random samples of TED Talks. A lower score indicates s is more like a sentence in weather forecast then in TED Talks.

5.1.2 Fine-tuning

In conventional fine-tuning, a NMT model is trained on a high-resource out-of-domain corpus until convergence, and then its parameters are fine-tuned on a low-resource in-domain corpus. We approach it in a slightly different way. Instead of training on out-of-domain corpus at the first step, we train on a shuffled combination of both in-domain and out-of-domain data, where the small-sized in-domain data may be copied several times, and the size of the out-of-domain data subset varies across experiments. This data size variation is intended to help us explore how different weighting and combination of data impacts final results.

5.2 Experimental Comparison

In order to evaluate the effectiveness of back-translation on low-resource gloss-text translation, we conduct experiments enhanced with data selection and fine-tuning techniques. We investigate the effect of data ratio by varying both the size of monolingual TED Talk data and the size of PHOENIX14T. For TED Talks, we adjust the cut-off threshold of the data selection score and result in 10k, 50k and 100k most relevant examples. For PHOENIX14T, as it is a tiny dataset,

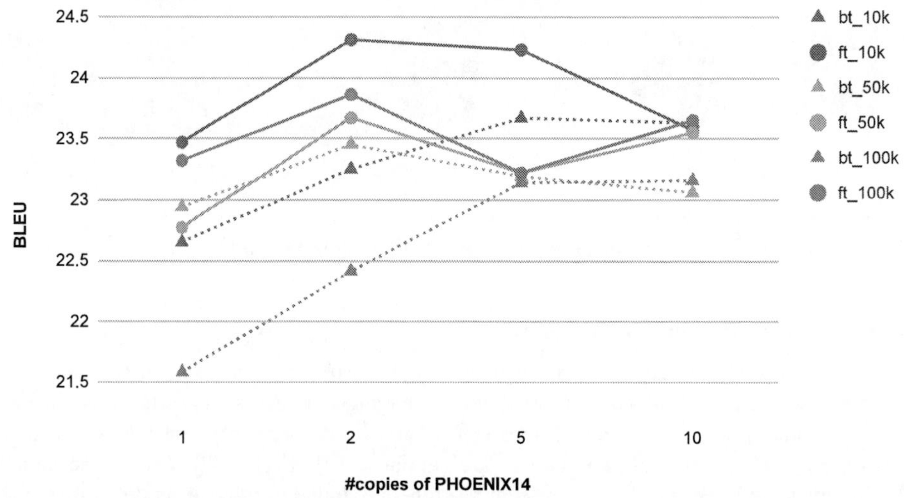

Figure 4: Performance of NMT systems on gloss-text translation. BLEU scores are evaluated on the test set of PHOENIX14T. Systems vary in whether fine-tuned on PHOENIX14T (bt vs. ft), the size of synthetic TED Talk data (10k, 50k, 100k) and the number of copies of PHOENIX14T added into the training data (0, 1, 2, 5, 10).

we simply balance the data ratio by making 0, 1, 2, 5 or 10 copies of it to combine with the synthetic TED Talk data. This new corpus is used to train a gloss-text system, which we call **bt** systems. Those systems are then fine-tuned on PHOENIX14T and result in **ft** systems.

5.3 Results on Out-Of-Domain Data Incorporation

We report the performance of different NMT systems in Figure 4.

Effect of fine-tuning Comparing **ft** to **bt** models, **ft** outperforms **bf** 10 out of 12 times. The improvement ranges from **0.03** BLEU to **1.74** BLEU, with an average of **0.7** BLEU. The largest improvement is achieved by **ft_100k_1**[6]. This shows that although the large amount of noisy out-of-domain data hurts the performance of the **bt** system, fine-tuning on only a small amount of in-domain data still improves the performance to a great extent.

Effect of data selection In order to evaluate the influence of data selection, we train two extra gloss-text systems and fine-tune them on PHOENIX14T. The difference is that system 1 uses randomly sampled TED data, while system 2 uses TED data selected by the Moore-Lewis method. It turns out that system 2 outperforms system 1 by 7.28 BLEU. Therefore, data selection is crucial when incorporating out-of-domain data in NMT.

Effect of the amount of out-of-domain data With the size of PHOENIX14T data fixed, **ft_10k** models are overall better than **ft_100k** models, which are better than **ft_50k** models. This is not the case for **bt** models, where **bt_100k** models tend to be worse than **bt_10k** and **bt_50k** models. This reveals one weakness of back-translation – it is prone to the quality of the

[6]This is short for a fine-tuned system that was trained on a concatenation of 100k TED data and 1 copy of PHOENIX14T data.

NMT System	BLEU
gloss-text_part1	19.13
text-gloss_part1	9.96
gloss-text_part1+synthetic part2	21.57

Table 2: Performance of NMT systems with in-domain monolingual data incorporation.

synthetic parallel data..

Effect of the amount of in-domain data Increasing the ratio of in-domain data in training data is not always beneficial – too much in-domain data might even hurts the performance. In practice, the data ratio can be taken as a tunable parameter and choose it wisely.

Effect of back-translation The best system enhanced with back-translation and domain adaptation techniques achieves **24.31** BLEU, which is slightly worse than the best BLEU score (**24.38**) achieved by hyperparameter search (Table 1). We wonder whether it would make a difference if the domain issue is eliminated. In next section, we simulate a condition when extra in-domain monolingual examples are available.

5.4 Results on In-Domain Data Incorporation

In order to evaluate back-translation on a less simpler situation, where domain mismatch is not a concern, we divide the PHOENIX14T training set into 2 parts. Each part contains 3,548 samples. We treat part 1 as a parallel corpus, while for part 2, we discard all the glosses and only keep the German text to simulate additional in-domain monolingual data.

We first train a gloss-text system on part 1 as a baseline (**gloss-text_part1**). Next, we train a text-gloss system on part 1 (**text-gloss_part1**). We then use this system to translate the German text from part 2 into synthetic glosses. The final gloss-text system is trained on the concatenation of part 1 and the synthetic parallel data of part 2 (**text-gloss_part1+synthetic part2**). The performance of the 3 systems on PHOENIX14T test set is shown in Table 2. The resulting gloss-text system improves over the baseline system by a margin of 2.44 BLEU. We can expect that given high-quality in-domain monolingual data, back-translation still has a great potential in improving the translation quality.

6 Conclusions

In this paper, we identify one challenging task in Sign Language Translation, that is the translation between sign language glosses and written languages. We argue that the obstacle lies in the sparsity of parallel data. To conquer this problem, we propose to approach sign language gloss translation as a low-resource machine translation task. We investigate the effectiveness of hyperparameter search and back-translation, which are both widely used by machine translation community for low-resource translations. We conclude that hyperparameter search is necessary, whereas back-translation is susceptible to the quality of additional monolingual data. If there is abundant in-domain monolingual data, back-translation is very promising. Otherwise, it should be used with domain adaptation techniques, like data selection and fine-tuning to achieve a reasonable performance.

Given limited parallel data, the upper bound of these low-resource methods is constrained. We thus urge the sign language processing community to put in extra efforts in creating more annotated parallel data.

References

Araabi, A. and Monz, C. (2020). Optimizing transformer for low-resource neural machine translation. *arXiv preprint arXiv:2011.02266.*

Camgoz, N. C., Hadfield, S., Koller, O., Ney, H., and Bowden, R. (2018). Neural sign language translation. In *2018 IEEE/CVF Conference on Computer Vision and Pattern Recognition.*

Camgöz, N. C., Kındıroğlu, A. A., and Akarun, L. (2016). Sign language recognition for assisting the deaf in hospitals. In Chetouani, M., Cohn, J., and Salah, A. A., editors, *Human Behavior Understanding.*

Camgoz, N. C., Koller, O., Hadfield, S., and Bowden, R. (2020). Sign language transformers: Joint end-to-end sign language recognition and translation. In *Proceedings of the IEEE/CVF Conference on Computer Vision and Pattern Recognition.*

Chu, C. and Wang, R. (2018). A survey of domain adaptation for neural machine translation. *arXiv preprint arXiv:1806.00258.*

Cui, R., Liu, H., and Zhang, C. (2017). Recurrent convolutional neural networks for continuous sign language recognition by staged optimization. In *Proceedings of the IEEE Conference on Computer Vision and Pattern Recognition (CVPR).*

Ding, S., Renduchintala, A., and Duh, K. (2019). A call for prudent choice of subword merge operations in neural machine translation. In *Proceedings of Machine Translation Summit XVII Volume 1: Research Track.*

Duh, K. (2018). The multitarget ted talks task. `http://www.cs.jhu.edu/~kevinduh/a/multitarget-tedtalks/`.

Duh, K., McNamee, P., Post, M., and Thompston, B. (2020). Benchmarking neural and statistical machine translationon low-resource african languages. In *Proceedings of the Language Resources and Evaluation Conference.*

Feldman, I. and Coto-Solano, R. (2020). Neural machine translation models with back-translation for the extremely low-resource indigenous language Bribri. In *Proceedings of the 28th International Conference on Computational Linguistics*, pages 3965–3976, Barcelona, Spain (Online). International Committee on Computational Linguistics.

Hieber, F., Domhan, T., Denkowski, M., Vilar, D., Sokolov, A., Clifton, A., and Post, M. (2017). Sockeye: A toolkit for neural machine translation. *arXiv preprint arXiv:1712.05690.*

Hoang, V. C. D., Koehn, P., Haffari, G., and Cohn, T. (2018). Iterative back-translation for neural machine translation. In *Proceedings of the 2nd Workshop on Neural Machine Translation and Generation*, pages 18–24, Melbourne, Australia. Association for Computational Linguistics.

Huang, J., Zhou, W., Zhang, Q., Li, H., and Li, W. (2018). Video-based sign language recognition without temporal segmentation. In *Proceedings of the AAAI Conference on Artificial Intelligence.*

Kingma, D. P. and Ba, J. (2014). Adam: A method for stochastic optimization. In *Proceedings of the 3rd International Conference on Learning Representations.*

Klein, A. and Hutter, F. (2019). Tabular benchmarks for joint architecture and hyperparameter optimization. *arXiv preprint arXiv:1905.04970.*

Ko, S.-K., Kim, C. J., Jung, H., and Cho, C. (2019). Neural sign language translation based on human keypoint estimation. *Applied Sciences*, 9(13):2683.

Koehn, P. (2020). *Neural Machine Translation.* Cambridge University Press.

Koehn, P., Hoang, H., Birch, A., Callison-Burch, C., Federico, M., Bertoldi, N., Cowan, B., Shen, W., Moran, C., Zens, R., et al. (2007). Moses: Open source toolkit for statistical machine translation. In *Proceedings of the 45th annual meeting of the ACL on interactive poster and demonstration sessions.*

Koehn, P. and Knowles, R. (2017). Six challenges for neural machine translation. In *Proceedings of the First Workshop on Neural Machine Translation.*

Koller, O., Zargaran, S., Ney, H., and Bowden, R. (2016). Deep sign: Hybrid cnn-hmm for continuous sign language recognition. In *BMVC.*

Kozik, K. (2019). Without sign language, deaf people are not equal.

Lample, G., Ott, M., Conneau, A., Denoyer, L., and Ranzato, M. (2018). Phrase-based & neural unsupervised machine translation. In *Proceedings of the 2018 Conference on Empirical Methods in Natural Language Processing*, pages 5039–5049, Brussels, Belgium. Association for Computational Linguistics.

Luong, T., Pham, H., and Manning, C. D. (2015). Effective approaches to attention-based neural machine translation. In *Proceedings of the 2015 Conference on Empirical Methods in Natural Language Processing.*

Moore, R. C. and Lewis, W. (2010). Intelligent selection of language model training data. In *Proceedings of the ACL 2010 conference short papers.*

Orbay, A. and Akarun, L. (2020). Neural sign language translation by learning tokenization. *arXiv preprint arXiv:2002.00479.*

Othman, A. and Jemni, M. (2012). English-asl gloss parallel corpus 2012: Aslg-pc12. In *5th Workshop on the Representation and Processing of Sign Languages: Interactions between Corpus and Lexicon LREC.*

Sennrich, R., Haddow, B., and Birch, A. (2016a). Improving neural machine translation models with monolingual data. In *Proceedings of the 54th Annual Meeting of the Association for Computational Linguistics (Volume 1: Long Papers).*

Sennrich, R., Haddow, B., and Birch, A. (2016b). Neural machine translation of rare words with subword units. In *Proceedings of the 54th Annual Meeting of the Association for Computational Linguistics (Volume 1: Long Papers).*

Sennrich, R. and Zhang, B. (2019). Revisiting low-resource neural machine translation: A case study. In *Proceedings of the 57th Annual Meeting of the Association for Computational Linguistics.*

Vaezi Joze, H. and Koller, O. (2019). Ms-asl: A large-scale data set and benchmark for understanding american sign language. In *The British Machine Vision Conference (BMVC).*

Valli, C., Lucas, C., Mulrooney, K. J., and Rankin, M. N. (2011). *Linguistics of American Sign Language: an introduction.* Gallaudet University Press.

Vaswani, A., Shazeer, N., Parmar, N., Uszkoreit, J., Jones, L., Gomez, A. N., Kaiser, L. u., and Polosukhin, I. (2017). Attention is all you need. In *Advances in Neural Information Processing Systems.*

Wang, H., Chai, X., Hong, X., Zhao, G., and Chen, X. (2016). Isolated sign language recognition with grassmann covariance matrices. *ACM Trans. Access. Comput.*

Yang, Z., Shi, Z., Shen, X., and Tai, Y. (2019). Sf-net: Structured feature network for continuous sign language recognition. *CoRR.*

Yin, F., Chai, X., and Chen, X. (2016). Iterative reference driven metric learning for signer independent isolated sign language recognition. In Leibe, B., Matas, J., Sebe, N., and Welling, M., editors, *European Conference on Computer Vision 2016.*

Yin, K. and Read, J. (2020). Better sign language translation with STMC-transformer. In *Proceedings of the 28th International Conference on Computational Linguistics.*

Zhang, X. and Duh, K. (2020). Reproducible and efficient benchmarks for hyperparameter optimization of neural machine translation systems. In *Transactions of the Association for Computational Linguistics.*

Zhang, X., Shapiro, P., Kumar, G., McNamee, P., Carpuat, M., and Duh, K. (2019). Curriculum learning for domain adaptation in neural machine translation. In *Proceedings of the 2019 Conference of the North American Chapter of the Association for Computational Linguistics: Human Language Technologies, Volume 1 (Long and Short Papers).*

Automatic generation of a 3D sign language avatar on AR glasses given 2D videos of human signers

Lan Thao Nguyen lan.t.nguyen@campus.tu-berlin.de
Florian Schicktanz
Technische Universität Berlin, Berlin, Germany

Aeneas Stankowski aeneas.stankowski@dfki.de
Eleftherios Avramidis eleftherios.avramidis@dfki.de
German Research Center for Artificial Intelligence (DFKI), Berlin, Germany

Abstract

In this paper we present a prototypical implementation of a pipeline that allows the automatic generation of a German Sign Language avatar from 2D video material. The presentation is accompanied by the source code. We record human pose movements during signing with computer vision models. The joint coordinates of hands and arms are imported as landmarks to control the skeleton of our avatar. From the anatomically independent landmarks, we create another skeleton based on the avatar's skeletal bone architecture to calculate the bone rotation data. This data is then used to control our human 3D avatar. The avatar is displayed on AR glasses and can be placed virtually in the room, in a way that it can be perceived simultaneously to the verbal speaker. In further work it is aimed to be enhanced with speech recognition and machine translation methods for serving as a sign language interpreter. The prototype has been shown to people of the deaf and hard-of-hearing community for assessing its comprehensibility. Problems emerged with the transferred hand rotations, hand gestures were hard to recognize on the avatar due to deformations like twisted finger meshes.

1 Introduction

About one million people in Europe are deaf and mainly communicate using sign language (SL), which consists of gestures of hands, arms and facial expressions. Outside their daily routines, deaf or hard-of-hearing (DHH) people face barriers for independently participating in society. The communication between signers and hearing speakers is often supported by trained SL interpreters. Beyond their respective communities, the availability of these services is often lacking or costly. New technological solutions may provide democratic alternatives to expensive and scarce translation resources and enable an independent communication between hearing and DHH people.

Our approach is based on the assumption that a simultaneous translation from spoken language to SL can enable more direct communication between deaf and hearing people. Through interviews with members of the DHH community, it was apparent that translations are understood even better when the interpreter's signs can be perceived with the speaker's mouth and gestures at the same time. If the person has a good picture of the mouth movement, around 30% of the speech can be read from the lips (Deutscher Gehörlosen-Bund e.V., 2021).

Several phases of the development were conducted with the support of members from the DHH community through a co-operation with the Center for Culture and Visual Communication of the Deaf in Berlin and Brandenburg (ZFK)[a] as described in our previous publication (Nguyen et al., 2021). In the discovery phase, qualitative interviews were conducted to provide user insights and lead the basic design decisions, including the choice of developing an avatar on AR glasses, as mentioned. In the early implementation phase, a professional deaf SL interpreter was video-recorded to provide material for the SL animation. In the evaluation phase, the efficacy of our proposed solution was evaluated via a wizard-of-Oz experiment, where a prototypical avatar was displayed in a way that it appeared as a fully developed automatic interpreter.

In this paper we focus on the technical implementation of this avatar. The 2D videos of the SL interpreter were analyzed with computer vision methods to extract human joint coordinates (landmarks). After mapping these landmarks on a pre-built avatar model, the virtual interpreter was displayed on a the AR glasses in the deaf person's field of view.

In the next chapter we give an overview of the related work. Chapter 3 provides the details about the implementation. In chapter 4 the evaluation process is described, whereas in chapter 5 we give a conclusion and indications for further research.

2 Related Work

In the last 30 years, diverse approaches to the automatic generation of SL have emerged. Tokuda and Okumura (1998) presented a prototype system for a word-to-word translation of Japanese to Japanese Sign Language (JSL) by finger spelling. By the beginning of the century, Elliott et al. (2000) specified the first framework for producing avatar based SL from text. They proposed the Signing Gesture Markup Language (SIGML; Elliott et al., 2004), an XML-formatted SL sequence description to drive the animation of an avatar in a web browser. It is built on the Hamburg Notation System (HamNoSys Hanke, 2004) that allows phonetic representations of signs.

SiGML is still applied in recent sign generation concepts (Kaur and Singh, 2015; Verma and Kaur, 2015; Rayner et al., 2016; Sugandhi et al., 2020). It is used as input language for the SL animation system Java Avatar Signing (JASigning) (Elliott et al., 2010), the successor of SiGMLSigning (Elliott et al., 2004). This was applied by Rayner et al. (2016) for their open online SL translation application development platform and Sugandhi et al. (2020), who developed a system that produces Indian Sign Language (ISL) from English text while considering ISL grammar. For the correct grammar they created a HamNoSys database before converting the representations to SiGML.

Another architecture was introduced by Heloir and Kipp (2010). They presented the Embodied Agents Behavior Realizer (EMBR) engine for robust real-time avatar animation. It is controlled by the EMBRScript which defines key poses for animation sequences. The EMBR system was later extended by Kipp et al. (2011) to build a sign animation tool based on a gloss database.

More similar to our approach, there is recent work that builds upon open source machine learning solutions which track human body keypoints from 2D video material. McConnell et al. (2020) animated a two-dimensional virtual human that is able to sign the British Sign Language (BSL) alphabet, based on body landmarks estimated by the OpenPose library (Cao et al., 2019). Although we also focus on a method requiring no special hardware or costly computing resources, we produce translations on a sentence level and we animate an avatar on all three dimensions.

Our work uses the three-dimensional landmark prediction of the lightweight and fast MediaPipe framework (Lugaresi et al., 2019). This was also considered for the automatic recognition of SL (Harditya, 2020; Chaikaew et al., 2021; Halder and Tayade, 2021; Bagby et al., 2021; Bansal et al., 2021) in previous work, but not for producing SL. MediaPipe is compatible

[a]Zentrum für Kultur und visuelle Kommunikation Gehörloser in Berlin & Brandenburg e.V., Potsdam, Germany

to more hardware systems and has less requirements than OpenPose. With the 2D skeleton generated by OpenPose and generative adversarial networks, Stoll et al. (2020) and Ventura et al. (2020) elaborated novel approaches to generate signing videos with photo realistic humans.

Regarding the animation of 3D avatars based on 2D recordings, Brock et al. (2020) developed a pipeline that creates skeletal data from sign videos with the help of multiple recurrent neural networks, proposing a new pose estimation framework specially designed for SL. The authors also compare the features of different available architectures, including OpenPose and MediaPipe. They provide a solution that covers all compared capabilities. To drive their avatar, angular and positional joint displacements are calculated with inverse kinematics, the results are then saved in a BVH file. User experiments showed that the synthesized avatar signing is comprehensible.

For this paper we implemented as a first step a more simplistic method, using an existing machine learning architecture and driving a virtual avatar by raw bone rotation data calculated in a 3D graphic suite. We are aiming to reach likewise comprehensibility results with a more refined animation approach in the future.

3 Implementation

The goal of the implementation was to create a SL avatar that is displayed in a HoloLens 1[b] and can be used for a proof of concept where we access the acceptability and comprehensibility of a simulated real-time translation on AR glasses among people from the DHH community.

Converting 2D SL video to a 3D avatar has multiple benefits (Kipp et al., 2011). In a simple use case, one can reside to this kind of conversion to create avatars out of pre-recorded SL speeches, while preserving the anonymity of the speakers. In a more advanced use case, such as the one of the automatic SL interpretation that we aim at, a big amount of sequences of SL gestures recorded from human speakers are required as graphical linguistic units. These will be used by a unified pipeline that generates full SL sentences, including methods of speech recognition and machine translation, to be implemented in further work. Collecting bigger amounts of human SL speaker recordings is aided if 2D cameras are used, as this is straightforward, does not require advanced equipment and allows using videos of different signers.

Our process of creating a SL avatar for AR glasses consists of four steps. First, we collected video footage of the predefined phrases by a professional interpreter (section 3.1). Then, based on the collected video footage, motion capture was used to convert the gestures and facial expressions into tracking points, using a motion tracking model that analyzes images and extracts body landmark positions (section 3.2). Based on the motion tracking points, the animations were transferred to the skeleton of the avatar after calculating rotation vectors (section 3.3). Finally, an application was developed to display the animated avatar on the AR glasses (section 3.4). The application, scripts and other material are published as open source.[cd]

3.1 Collection of video material

We filmed a professional deaf interpreter translating written German sentences to German Sign Language (Deutsche Gebärdensprache; DGS). Since this footage is needed to track all human joint landmarks in every single video frame, it was necessary to capture high-resolution video with as few motion blur as possible. Using a single-lens reflex camera, this was achieved by setting a very short exposure time of 1/1600, a relatively low f-number of 2.8 and a very high ISO value of 3200 for strong light sensitivity. Moreover, a 1920x1080 full HD resolution and a frame rate of 25 FPS were chosen. The recording took place at a professional film studio of the

[b]https://docs.microsoft.com/de-de/hololens/hololens1-hardware

[c]https://github.com/lanthaon/sl-animation-blender

[d]https://github.com/lanthaon/sl-roleplay-unity

ZFK, where translations for the public TV are recorded as well. The recording lasted 4 hours and was supported by a professional film team. Three cameras filmed the interpretation from 3 different angles, but in this paper we only use the frontal camera. We will consider using the full footage including the side cameras in order to improve detection precision in future work.

3.2 Generating Motion Capture Data

The footage was processed with a pipeline integrating three machine learning models for computer vision that analyze the images and generate body landmarks with 3D coordinates for the upper body, hands and face. These are depicted in image A of figure 1. Face detection combines a compact feature extractor convolutional neural network with the anchor scheme of the Single Shot Multibox Detector (Liu et al., 2016; Bazarevsky et al., 2019). The upper body was analyzed via a body pose tracking model that uses an encoder-decoder heatmap-based network and a subsequent regression encoder network (Bazarevsky et al., 2020). The hands were analyzed with a palm detector, combined with a hand landmark detection model via multi-view bootstrapping (Simon et al., 2017; Zhang et al., 2020).

We used the tools including the pre-trained models of MediaPipe Holistic (Grishchenko and Bazarevsky, 2020) and wrote a Python script for the open source 3D graphic suite *Blender version 2.91.2*[e] to create exportable motion capture data based on the landmarks. For the scripting, we worked with the *Blender Python module*, *MediaPipe version 0.8.3.1* and *OpenCV version 4.5.1.48* under *Python 3.7*.

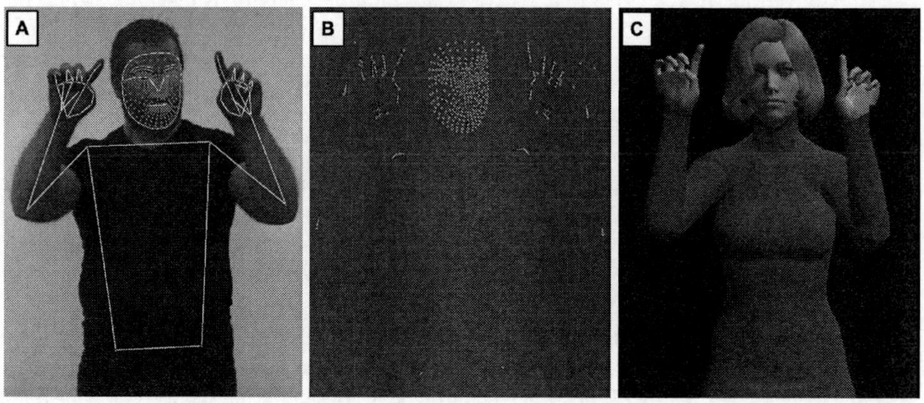

Figure 1: Holistic tracking applied to a video frame. A) is the annotated original footage where the red dots are the tracked landmarks, while the green lines connect the joints. B) is the same frame in Blender with landmarks plotted as orange spheres and cyan coloured bones. C) shows the motion capture data applied to an avatar.

In order to extract the landmarks frame by frame, we created the method `get_video_frames` that splits the video into an array of frames. It passes a video file URL as string to the `VideoCapture` class of OpenCV, which then decodes the video frames.

The resulting frame list can then be used in method `get_landmarks`. Within the function, a for-loop is called which iterates the frame array, calculates the landmarks with MediaPipe Holistic and saves them for each frame and type into the corresponding arrays for pose, left hand, right hand and face. In the optimal case, after the last iteration the arrays should contain n lists of tracked landmarks, where n is the number of frames. If for example the left

[e]https://www.blender.org/download/releases/2-91/

Mesh type	*Polygon count*
Hair	13.035
Shoes	4808
Dress	149.122
Shape	16.720
Total	183.685 < 200.000

Table 1: Polygon count of the avatar mesh divided into categories

hand could not be tracked in the first frame, a `NoneType` object is added to the array instead of a landmark list.

After gathering the landmarks into arrays, they can be passed to `load_landmarks_into_scene`. While iterating the specified landmark array, sphere objects are created once for each existing landmark and are named uniquely after their corresponding MediaPipe landmark model designation. To update the spheres' locations analogous to the video frame, keyframes are set in each iteration. The XYZ coordinates are multiplied with a factor of either 30 or 40 to stretch the distances between the points, enabling to better analyze the results visually. Image B in figure 1 shows the landmark cloud, highlighted in orange, for an exemplary keyframe.

The last step is to built an armature with bones based on the animated landmark cloud which is done in method `create_bones`. For this, lists of string tuples with names of start and target landmarks were defined to specify between which two landmarks a bone should be created. The first tuple item is the name of the start landmark. There, the bone's root will be located. The second item is the target landmark that determines the direction to where the bone's end joint should point at. These rules were implemented as bone constraints to which the bones adapt automatically in each keyframe.

Finally, the resulting skeleton was exported as a Biovision Hierarchy (BVH) file, which is a common file type for motion capture data. After that, the next step was to apply the animation data in the BVH file to a 3D character, like depicted in C of figure 1. This will be described further in the following subsection.

3.3 Creating and animating the avatar

For the creation of the 3D avatar, the 3D modelling software *Daz Studio*[f] has been used. The Daz community provides free 3D content as well as 3D content for a fee. Only free 3D content has been chosen for the character shape and assets like hair, cloth and shoes. To work with the character in Blender, it has been exported with the *Daz to Blender Bridge*[g].

When developing apps for the HoloLens, it should be considered that the device is a self-contained computer with the processing power of a mobile phone. It is recommended to limit the overall polygon count to under 200,000 faces. We could keep the polygon count under this level by choosing less elaborately designed assets. The number of faces for each asset are summarized in Table 1.

3D characters created in Daz are fully rigged and prepared for animation purposes. The character's bone structure has been analyzed to figure out the important upper body bones to which our BVH skeleton had to be adjusted. To apply the produced BVH data, both the character and the BVH armature were imported into a Blender scene. In a Python script we defined the matching bone pairs between their skeletons and set bone constraints on the

[f]https://www.daz3d.com/get_studio

[g]https://www.daz3d.com/daz-to-blender-bridge

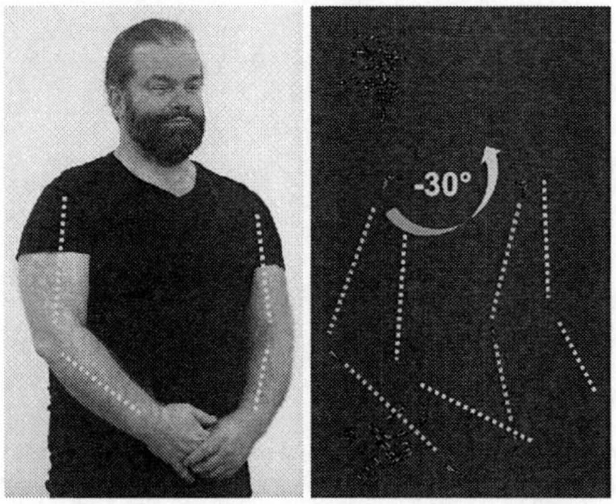

Figure 2: Original video frame compared to BVH skeleton based on MediaPipe tracking. The arms have a narrower angle than the original, while hands and face were tracked properly. Starting from a perfect vertical alignment, a more natural orientation was achieved by rotating the skeleton -30° along the corresponding axis.

avatar to copy the rotation of the assigned BVH bones. In listing 1 is an example variable `pose_bones_mapping` that defines the mapping for the arm rotations calculated based on the pose landmarks. The left entries are the bone names from the motion capture skeleton, the right entries bone names from the Daz avatar. We named the BVH bones after their target landmark.

Listing 1: Variable defining matching arm bones between the Daz avatar skeleton and the BVH armature

```
pose_bones_mapping = [
    ("LEFT_ELBOW", "lShldrBend"),
    ("LEFT_WRIST", "lForearmBend"),
    ("RIGHT_ELBOW", "rShldrBend"),
    ("RIGHT_WRIST", "rForearmBend")
]
```

Analyzing the resulting motion capture data in Blender revealed that hand, arm and face landmarks were not tracked coherently by MediaPipe, they rather seemed disconnected from each other. In figure 2 the face, arm and hand positions produced by the machine learning solution can be compared to the original recorded person. While hands and face seem to have proper results, the arms appear to be angled narrower which indicates an inaccurate depth estimation. Since our method copies only bone rotations and not bone positions, no full alignment is necessary, but the skeleton had to be adjusted due to the unnatural orientation of the arms before applying the rotations to the avatar. This was solved by writing a short function that adapts the global rotation for the BVH skeleton as visualized on the right image of figure 2.

The mapping of the bone rotations was done in method `map_bones` which iterates through all bone pairs of a tuple list like in listing 1. There the rotations from the BVH armature in the scene are to copied to the avatar's bones. In general, all XYZ axes are considered for copying the rotation, except for the head and neck bones, where the y axis is excluded. Because there was still the problem of the too narrow arm angle, the influence of the rotation copy constraint for the forearm bone has been reduced. In some animations the avatar's forearms or the hands would otherwise penetrate other body parts like the face.

For the proof of concept, only rotations for arms, hand and experimentally XZ rotations for head and neck bones were transferred to the avatar. The implementation of facial expressions constitutes additional challenges that have to be taken on in future work, since they represent an essential element of the SL. Head and neck bones were created between specific face bones, but in principle, no tracking landmarks exist for the posture.

To continue with the development of the HoloLens application, the animated avatar was exported as a Filmbox (FBX) file that can be imported by the required Unity game engine[h].

3.4 HoloLens Application Development

We used *Unity version 2019.4.20f1 (LTS)* for the development together with *Microsoft's Mixed Reality Toolkit (MRTK) for Unity version 2.5.3*[i]. The toolkit provides a bounding box into which we embedded our avatar, enabling to position, rotate and scale the virtual character in space. With this feature we could place the avatar independently of the environment in a way that the study participant could see both the speaking person and the virtual interpreter avatar. To avoid that the 3D character is accidentally moved somewhere else during the user study, we implemented a virtual start button that disables the bounding box control before reaching the AR glasses to our participants.

An additional physical clicker that connects to the HoloLens 1 via Bluetooth allowed us to trigger actions during the study without wearing the AR glasses ourselves. The main camera's pointer handler of the Unity scene listens to the global event *On Pointer Clicked.* When this event occurs, a method is called that plays the next animation defined in a list containing the 3D avatar's motion clip names.

After our first application prototype we experienced that the AR glasses' computational limits were exceeded when more than ten avatars had to be handled, whereby each of them signed a different sentence. App size and computational complexity increased due to the many objects to a level that the HoloLens could not handle. It crashed each time after starting the app. Thus, our solution was to merge all animation clips needed for the role play in the user study into one avatar. The Unity app was finally deployed on the HoloLens with the *Community Edition of Visual Studio 2019*[j]. Figure 3 illustrates how the avatar was positioned in the study room.

Figure 3: Final user test setup. A participant (left) is wearing a HoloLens 1 displaying a virtual avatar in front of the table by the impersonated doctor (right), while a sign interpreter (middle) is prepared to translate the participant's feedback.

[h] https://unity.com/de

[i] https://docs.microsoft.com/de-de/windows/mixed-reality/mrtk-unity/

[j] https://visualstudio.microsoft.com/de/vs/

4 Evaluation

Our evaluation comprised a user study and discovery phase prior to the implementation (Nguyen et al., 2021). In the discovery phase we reached out to the Center for Culture and Visual Communication of the Deaf in Berlin and Brandenburg (ZFK), which is a major contact point for deaf people in the area. Four qualitative interviews were conducted and recorded to gather insights about the DHH communities' needs.

We could identify doctor appointments as a difficult situation for deaf people without an interpreter. Additionally, the interviewees rated different mock-ups, showing three translation options on three different technical devices. AR glasses combined with a virtual avatar were considered as one of the two most useful options. The option of having a live interpreter displayed in AR glasses was rated as equally helpful, yet would only slightly improve the status quo, as it would make such service locally dependent and the limited availability of interpreters still remains a problem.

To test the prototype system, we conducted a user study similar to a wizard-of-Oz-experiment (Nguyen et al., 2021). The use case of a medical examination was chosen during which the doctor asks the patient several questions. In that context, an examination dialog with predefined sentences was written and translated to SL. In the context of the dialog, the doctor is expecting certain reactions from the DHH patient, which decrease the risk of wrong understanding e.g. *"Show me, where you do have pain?"*. One of the experiment supervisors performed the role of the doctor and read aloud the prepared sentences, while another supervisor used an external clicker to trigger the corresponding animations on the AR glasses that were worn by the participants. Speech recognition will have to be integrated in future implementations for an independent live translation system.

We are conscious that medical usage requires high precision which is hard to be achieved by the state of the art. Nevertheless, we proceeded with this case for the experiment, since it was suggested during the discovery phase interviews as one of high importance for the users' community and could therefore motivate better the evaluation of the full concept.

The whole scene was filmed and a survey of standardized questions was asked at the end of a user test. Additional information about the qualitative results may be found in the prior published report (Nguyen et al., 2021).

Among the three female and five male participants from which six were deaf, there were also one hearing and one hard-of-hearing person. Results showed a high acceptance rate of the presented solution, even though the comprehensibility of the avatar's signing was rather low. Participants had difficulties to identify the movements of the fingers, as the actual positions of the individual finger joints were harder to distinguish through the often warped or deformed hand mesh. Sometimes the movements of the avatar's hands were furthermore jittery or incorrect due to technical reasons concerning the fidelity of the implementation. Besides, the study participants felt affected by the missing lip movements and facial expressions, which are relevant for performing grammatical functions. For example, raising the eyebrows indicates a question in DGS. With the chosen level of quality the purpose of conducting a proof of concept was achieved, but can be improved in the future.

To summarize, sentences that were signed mainly with finger movements showed a poorer comprehensibility rate than sentences with prominent arm movements that relied less on specific hand gestures. Although the arms seem to have been tracked less accurately than the hands, after being transferred to the avatar their movements were easier to recognize than finger movements, as the overall size and length of the movements mitigate the lower landmark precision. The mesh of the avatar's fingers was often deformed or twisted after copying the rotation of a bone created between two MediaPipe landmarks. We assume that the approach needs to be optimized mathematically, since the bone rotations calculated automatically with Blender are not a fully accurate solution to generate SL from 2D videos. In addition, there were some inaccuracies in the depth data estimated by MediaPipe, which led to altered distances between different parts of the body, like hands and face. Also, the spine is not tracked, thus the posture of the avatar cannot be influenced yet if for example the head is shifted forward in the video.

5 Conclusion

We developed a method to generate SL from 2D video recordings with the help of machine learning methods of computer vision and a 3D creation suite. A skeleton was built from the detected body landmarks by creating bones between pairs of specified landmarks. This was then exported as BVH data and applied to a rigged avatar. The avatar's bone constraints were set to copy the rotations of the matching bones from the BVH skeleton.

Some problems became apparent after mapping the bone rotations to the avatar. Besides modified distances between hands or arms to the body, the most severe issue was the twisting of the finger meshes which altered their appearance significantly. The user study with our prototype system showed that the avatar's hand gestures were hard to recognize for most participants. This led to poorer comprehensibility for sentences where the attention had to be paid predominantly to the finger movements, while sentences with discernible arm movements were recognized by the majority.

As it has been noted, the animation approach needs to be optimized to achieve more comprehensible results. Facial expressions and if possible lip movements should be enabled in future implementations. Still, a high acceptance level could be observed for the concept of displaying a SL avatar in AR glasses. We believe that a well developed automated speech to SL system could enable more freedom and flexibility for deaf people in situations where an interpretation can enhance communication significantly, but would be normally not affordable due to the scarce availability of interpreters.

Even if our prototype system for the experiment is static through the predefined, manually triggered questions, it opens the door for several use cases where content and vocabulary are restricted, e.g. a museum tour. Moreover, it was important for us to create an animation solution that requires no special hardware and enables other researchers as well as non-professionals an open-source tool for producing three-dimensional virtually performed SL with an avatar. Our vision is to create the basis for an animation data-set which can grow with the addition of more scenarios and can be used for the further development of a system allowing the real-time translation of arbitrary conversations, in conjunction with methods from speech recognition and machine translation.

Acknowledgements

This research was supported by Uwe Schönfeld, Mathias Schäfer, Helene Sudermann, Lukas Gesche, Johann Carl Reischies, Marco Richardson and Willi Reuter. It has been accomplished as a semester project at the Technische Universität Berlin, hosted by the Quality and Usability Lab and organized by Neslihan Iskender under the chair of Prof. Sebastian Möller. Supervision from the side of DFKI has been supported by the project SocialWear (Socially Interactive Smart Fashion) funded by the German Ministry of Education (BMBF), with the support of Fabrizio Nunnari and Esther Zahn.

References

Bagby, B., Gray, D., Hughes, R., Langford, Z., and Stonner, R. (2021). Simplifying sign language detection for smart home devices using google mediapipe. https://bradenbagby.com/Portfolio/Resources/PDFs/ResearchPaper.pdf.

Bansal, D., Ravi, P., So, M., Agrawal, P., Chadha, I., Murugappan, G., and Duke, C. (2021). Copycat: Using sign language recognition to help deaf children acquire language skills. In *Extended Abstracts of the 2021 CHI Conference on Human Factors in Computing Systems*, pages 1–10.

Bazarevsky, V., Grishchenko, I., Raveendran, K., Zhu, T., Zhang, F., and Grundmann, M. (2020). BlazePose: On-device Real-time Body Pose tracking. *CoRR*, abs/2006.1.

Bazarevsky, V., Kartynnik, Y., Vakunov, A., Raveendran, K., and Grundmann, M. (2019). BlazeFace: Sub-millisecond Neural Face Detection on Mobile GPUs. *CoRR*, abs/1907.0.

Brock, H., Law, F., Nakadai, K., and Nagashima, Y. (2020). Learning three-dimensional skeleton data from sign language video. *ACM Trans. Intell. Syst. Technol.*, 11(3).

Cao, Z., Hidalgo, G., Simon, T., Wei, S.-E., and Sheikh, Y. (2019). Openpose: realtime multi-person 2d pose estimation using part affinity fields. *IEEE transactions on pattern analysis and machine intelligence*, 43(1):172–186.

Chaikaew, A., Somkuan, K., and Yuyen, T. (2021). Thai sign language recognition: an application of deep neural network. In *2021 Joint International Conference on Digital Arts, Media and Technology with ECTI Northern Section Conference on Electrical, Electronics, Computer and Telecommunication Engineering*, pages 128–131.

Deutscher Gehörlosen-Bund e.V. (2021). Wie viele Gehörlose gibt es in Deutschland? https://www.gehoerlosen-bund.de/faq/geh%C3%B6rlosigkeit.

Elliott, R., Bueno, J., Kennaway, R., and Glauert, J. (2010). Towards the integration of synthetic sl animation with avatars into corpus annotation tools. In *4th Workshop on the Representation and Processing of Sign Languages: Corpora and Sign Language Technologies, Valletta, Malta*, page 29.

Elliott, R., Glauert, J. R., Jennings, V., and Kennaway, J. (2004). An overview of the sigml notation and sigmlsigning software system. In *Fourth International Conference on Language Resources and Evaluation, LREC*, pages 98–104.

Elliott, R., Glauert, J. R. W., Kennaway, J. R., and Marshall, I. (2000). The development of language processing support for the visicast project. In *Proceedings of the Fourth International ACM Conference on Assistive Technologies*, Assets '00, page 101–108, New York, NY, USA. Association for Computing Machinery.

Grishchenko, I. and Bazarevsky, V. (2020). MediaPipe Holistic — Simultaneous Face, Hand and Pose Prediction, on Device. http://ai.googleblog.com/2020/12/mediapipe-holistic-simultaneous-face.html.

Halder, A. and Tayade, A. (2021). Real-time vernacular sign language recognition using mediapipe and machine learning. *International Journal of Research Publication and Reviews*, 2(5):9–17.

Hanke, T. (2004). Hamnosys-representing sign language data in language resources and language processing contexts. In *LREC*, volume 4, pages 1–6.

Harditya, A. (2020). Indonesian sign language (bisindo) as means to visualize basic graphic shapes using teachable machine. In *International Conference of Innovation in Media and Visual Design (IMDES 2020)*, pages 1–7. Atlantis Press.

Heloir, A. and Kipp, M. (2010). Real-time animation of interactive agents: Specification and realization. *Applied Artificial Intelligence*, 24(6):510–529.

Kaur, S. and Singh, M. (2015). Indian sign language animation generation system. In *2015 1st International Conference on Next Generation Computing Technologies (NGCT)*, pages 909–914. IEEE.

Kipp, M., Heloir, A., and Nguyen, Q. (2011). Sign language avatars: Animation and comprehensibility. In Vilhjálmsson, H. H., Kopp, S., Marsella, S., and Thórisson, K. R., editors, *Intelligent Virtual Agents*, pages 113–126. Springer Berlin Heidelberg.

Liu, W., Anguelov, D., Erhan, D., Szegedy, C., Reed, S., Fu, C. Y., and Berg, A. C. (2016). SSD: Single shot multibox detector. In *Lecture Notes in Computer Science (including subseries Lecture Notes in Artificial Intelligence and Lecture Notes in Bioinformatics)*, volume 9905 LNCS, pages 21–37. Springer Verlag.

Lugaresi, C., Tang, J., Nash, H., McClanahan, C., Uboweja, E., Hays, M., Zhang, F., Chang, C.-L., Yong, M. G., Lee, J., Chang, W.-T., Hua, W., Georg, M., and Grundmann, M. (2019). Mediapipe: A framework for building perception pipelines.

McConnell, M., Foster, M. E., and Ellen, M. (2020). Two Dimensional Sign Language Agent. In *Proceedings of the 20th ACM International Conference on Intelligent Virtual Agents*, New York, NY, USA. ACM.

Nguyen, L. T., Schicktanz, F., Stankowski, A., and Avramidis, E. (2021). Evaluating the translation of speech to virtually-performed sign language on ar glasses. In *Proceedings of the Thirteenth International Conference on Quality of Multimedia Experience (QoMEX). International Conference on Quality of Multimedia Experience (QoMEX-2021), June 14-17*. IEEE.

Rayner, E., Bouillon, P., Gerlach, J., Strasly, I., Tsourakis, N., and Ebling, S. (2016). An openweb platform for rule-based speech-to-sign translation. In *54th annual meeting of the Association for Computational Linguistics (ACL)*.

Simon, T., Joo, H., Matthews, I., and Sheikh, Y. (2017). Hand Keypoint Detection in Single Images using Multiview Bootstrapping. In *Proceedings of the IEEE Conference on Computer Vision and Pattern Recognition (CVPR)*, pages 1145–1153.

Stoll, S., Camgoz, N. C., Hadfield, S., and Bowden, R. (2020). Text2Sign: Towards Sign Language Production Using Neural Machine Translation and Generative Adversarial Networks. *International Journal of Computer Vision*, 128(4):891–908.

Sugandhi, Kumar, P., and Kaur, S. (2020). Sign Language Generation System Based on Indian Sign Language Grammar. *ACM Transactions on Asian and Low-Resource Language Information Processing*, 19(4):1–26.

Tokuda, M. and Okumura, M. (1998). Towards automatic translation from japanese into japanese sign language. In *Assistive Technology and Artificial Intelligence*, pages 97–108. Springer.

Ventura, L., Duarte, A., and i Nieto, X. G. (2020). Can Everybody Sign Now? Exploring Sign Language Video Generation from 2D Poses. In *ECCV 2020 Workshop on Sign Language recognition, Production and Translation (SLRTP)*.

Verma, A. and Kaur, S. (2015). Indian sign language animation generation system for gurumukhi script. *International Journal of Computer Science and Technology*, 6(3):117–121.

Zhang, F., Bazarevsky, V., Vakunov, A., Tkachenka, A., Sung, G., Chang, C.-L., and Grundmann, M. (2020). MediaPipe Hands: On-device Real-time Hand Tracking. *CoRR*, abs/2006.1.

Online Evaluation of Text-to-sign Translation by Deaf End Users: Some Methodological Recommendations

Floris Roelofsen f.roelofsen@uva.nl
Lyke Esselink l.d.esselink@uva.nl
Shani Mende-Gillings s.e.mendegillings@uva.nl
University of Amsterdam, the Netherlands

Maartje de Meulder maartje.demeulder@hu.nl
Nienke Sijm nienke.sijm@hu.nl
Utrecht University for Applied Sciences, the Netherlands

Anika Smeijers a.s.smeijers@amsterdamumc.nl
Amsterdam University Medical Centre, the Netherlands

Abstract

We present a number of methodological recommendations concerning the online evaluation of avatars for text-to-sign translation, focusing on the structure, format and length of the questionnaire, as well as methods for eliciting and faithfully transcribing responses.

1 Introduction

There is no generally accepted methodology for evaluating the comprehensibility of avatars for text-to-sign translation, let alone for doing so *online*. Evaluation procedures designed in previous work generally involve on-site interaction between experimenters and participants (Gibet et al. 2011; Smith and Nolan 2016; Ebling and Glauert 2016; David and Bouillon 2018; Huenerfauth 2006; Kacorri et al. 2015, though see Quandt et al. 2021 and Schnepp et al. 2011 for exceptions). The COVID-19 pandemic has made it necessary to turn to online procedures, which come with additional methodological challenges. On the bright side, such online procedures, if effective, may also have benefits in a post-COVID-19 world.

We report work in progress on the evaluation of a recently developed prototype system for translating sentences that frequently occur in a healthcare setting, particularly ones that are used in the diagnosis and treatment of COVID-19, from Dutch into Dutch Sign Language (NGT). The system itself is described in some detail in Roelofsen et al. (2021). Here, we share some of the lessons we have learned in designing a methodology for evaluating this system online. Some of these lessons specifically concern the online nature of the evaluation procedure, but others are more general and would apply to on-site evaluation as well.

In the process of designing our methodology, we held a feedback session with seven deaf researchers at various career stages, all users of NGT and familiar with (socio-)linguistic experimental methodologies, in which we discussed a preliminary setup of the evaluation procedure. After incorporating feedback from this session we carried out a pilot study with five participants (all consider NGT (one of) their mother tongue(s)). While the feedback session had already led to important improvements of the design, the pilot study brought out a number of further methodological issues, serious enough to render the results essentially uninterpretable. To address these issues, we have further adapted the design of the evaluation procedure, which is described in more detail in Section 4. The adapted procedure is already in use. Although it is too early to present quantified results, it is clear that the methodological adjustments we made are effective, as the issues experienced in the pilot study are no longer present. By sharing the lessons we have learned from the feedback session and the pilot study, we hope that other researchers evaluating avatars for text-to-sign translation in the future, be it online or on-site, will be able to avoid making the same mistakes we did initially and arrive at a suitable evaluation procedure more directly.

The extended abstract is organised as follows: Section 2 outlines the goals of our evaluation procedure, Section 3 discusses the design of the questionnaire, Section 4 turns to issues concerning elicitation and transcription of participants' responses, and Section 5 concludes.

2 Evaluation goals

As mentioned above, the system we are evaluating translates sentences that frequently occur in a healthcare setting, especially in the diagnosis and treatment of COVID-19, from Dutch to NGT. For instance, a healthcare professional may enter the sentence 'Gebruikt u medicijnen?' ('Do you use any medications?') and the system will produce a translation in NGT. Some translations have been pre-recorded on video, others are displayed by means of an avatar, making use of the JASigning avatar software (Kennaway et al., 2007; Ebling and Glauert, 2016). We are mainly interested at this point in evaluating the comprehensibility of these avatar translations.

More specifically, our primary goal currently is to answer the following three questions:

1. **Individual sign recognition**: To what extent do deaf NGT users recognise the individual signs that the avatar translations consist of?
2. **Sentence comprehension**: To what extent do deaf NGT users understand the avatar translations as intended at sentence level?
3. **Clarity**: How clear are the avatar translations that the system produces?

Measuring individual sign recognition alongside sentence comprehension provides us with additional insights as to *why* a sentence is (mis)understood, and highlights specific areas for improvement. For example, some participants may recognise individual signs yet misidentify the meaning of a sentence (or vice versa).

A secondary goal (equally important in general, but less central in the present study) is to find out how members of the deaf community in the Netherlands view avatar technology for sign language translation, and the potential application of such technology in various domains (cf., David and Bouillon 2018; Bouillon et al. 2021; Quandt et al. 2021, among others).

3 Design of the questionnaire

We will comment on three design features of the questionnaire: its structure, format, and length.

Structure In evaluating the comprehensibility of avatar translations, it is crucial to have a standard of comparison. Suppose, for instance, that we find that users correctly recognise 75% of the individual signs that the avatar produces. This information in itself does not tell us much. Is this a positive result, or a negative one? We cannot tell as long as we do not have a baseline. This concern is particularly relevant here for two reasons. First, some of the translations involve medical terms (e.g., 'intravenous drip') which may not be familiar to all participants and therefore poorly recognised even if they are signed correctly by the avatar. Second, there is considerable regional and intergenerational variation in NGT, which means that certain signs may be familiar to NGT users from one region/generation, but not to users from another. To address this issue, we compare the comprehensibility of avatar translations to that of video recordings of the same sentences signed by a deaf signer. The core of the questionnaire, then, consists of two parts: one that assesses the comprehensibility of avatar translations, and one that does the same for baseline videos signed by a deaf signer. The avatar part precedes the baseline part, to avoid a learning effect when assessing the avatar.

After these two core comprehension parts, the questionnaire inquires about the participant's general perception of avatar technology for sign language translation, and their views on the potential application of such technology in various domains.

In addition, the questionnaire includes an introductory part (informed consent, information about the structure of the questionnaire, and some questions about the language background of the participants) and a closing part which checks whether the questions in the questionnaire were clearly posed and could be responded to in a satisfactory way.

Format All questions and instructions in the questionnaire are presented both in NGT (by means of pre-recorded videos) and in written Dutch. The person giving instructions and asking questions in the videos is a deaf NGT user, distinct from the signer in the baseline video translations discussed above. Participants are given a choice as to whether they want to watch the questions/instructions in NGT, read the Dutch text, or both. Most participants preferred the videos, but some chose to read. Several participants explicitly commented that they appreciated having this choice. Some explicitly commented that they found it pleasant that the person in the video was a deaf signer. All participants reported that the questions and instructions were clear.

Length We aim to keep sessions under 45 minutes to avoid concentration difficulties. This seems to work well—participants appear to be focused all the way through. What we have learned, however, is that this means that the number of test sentences has to be kept quite low. Our initial plan was to present 24 avatar translations and 24 corresponding baseline videos, but this turned out not to be feasible at all. We now present 12 avatar translations and 12 baseline videos, and this generally fits the 45 minute window.

Another lesson we learned is that, in order to measure the extent to which the individual signs in a sentence are correctly recognised, the length of test sentences should be restricted to around 7 signs. It is well-known that most adults cannot store more than 7 items in their short-term memory (Miller, 1956). Indeed, when we presented longer sentences in our pilot study and asked participants to list the individual signs in these sentences, they had great trouble reproducing the right sequence even if they had fully understood the meaning of the sentence as a whole. Since our aim here is not to test participants' short term memory capacity but just comprehension, we have decided to keep all test sentences relatively short (4-7 signs). In the evaluation sessions we are currently running this appears to work well.

4 Eliciting and transcribing responses

For a proper evaluation procedure (ensuring that responses are correctly understood by all parties), the responses that participants provide in NGT have to be simultaneously interpreted into Dutch. This is not straightforward if, as in our case, the experimenters are not fluent signers: one is a new signer using NGT on a daily basis and the other has taken a number of NGT courses but does not use the language daily. The online setting makes this issue even more acute. We are addressing this issue as follows. During an evaluation session, the participant does not open the questionnaire on their own computer. Rather, one of the experimenters opens the questionnaire on their computer and shares their screen. An experienced sign language interpreter, with high awareness of regional and generational variation, is present as well. Before getting started, we make sure that both the questionnaire and the sign language interpreter are visible for the participant. Participants answer questions in NGT, i.e., they do not need to type anything themselves.

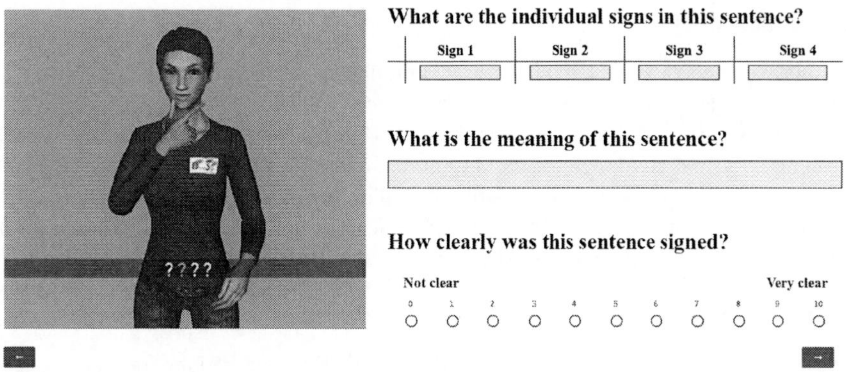

Figure 1: An example of an item in the questionnaire assessing comprehension of the avatar. For illustration, the questions are formulated in English here; in reality they are in Dutch and accompanied by instructions in NGT.

The interpreter interprets the answers into Dutch, one of the experimenters types the verbatim interpretation visible for the participants, so that they can check that their responses are properly interpreted. Typically, participants correct interpretations a few times each session and the transcript is then changed accordingly. In other cases, participants typically indicate explicitly that the interpretation is correct (usually with a confirming head nod after the transcription appears on the screen).

Finally, we turn to the issue of how to properly assess the extent to which participants recognise the *individual signs* in the avatar translations. This issue is more specific than the ones discussed above, but needs to be carefully addressed in any study that evaluates the comprehension of signing avatars. Indeed, the data obtained in our pilot study was uninterpretable mostly because we had not addressed this issue carefully enough.

In the pilot study, we gave participants instructions (both in NGT and in written Dutch) that they would be shown a video of an avatar signing a sentence and would then be asked three questions (i) What are the individual signs in the sentence? (ii) What is the meaning of the sentence as a whole? and (iii) How clearly was the sentence signed? Next, we showed participants a video, and then questions (i)-(iii), in Dutch. Responses to the first two questions (individual signs and sentence meaning) had to be entered in a textfield, while responses to the third question (clarity) had to be given on a scale from 0 to 10. The problem was that participants generally (with very few exceptions in fact) immediately started answering the second question. It was not sufficiently clear what was intended with the first question.

We took two measures to address this issue. First, rather than a single textfield for listing the individual signs in the sentence, we now present a separate textfield for each sign and label these textfields as 'Sign 1', 'Sign 2', etc (see Figure 1). Second, when giving instructions beforehand we now present two examples: one of an avatar translation with 'gloss subtitles', where the item in the gloss that corresponds to the current sign gets highlighted in yellow, and a second example of an avatar translation with question marks in the subtitles (see Figure 1). During the first sign the first question mark is highlighted, during the second sign the second question mark etc. Together with this second example video we also show the first two questions (concerning individual signs and sentence meaning, respectively), and exemplify what a possible response could look like. The question mark subtitles are also included in the actual test items. These two revisions of the design appear to achieve the intended effect: in the evaluation procedure we are currently running participants so far respond to all questions as intended.

5 Conclusion

In this extended abstract, we have shared a number of methodological lessons we have learned in designing and piloting an online procedure to evaluate the comprehensibility of an avatar for text-to-sign translation. We hope that the recommendations we have made concerning the structure, format, and length of the questionnaire and test items, as well as the elicitation and transcription of responses will be helpful for other researchers in designing their evaluation procedures. In the long run, we hope that they contribute to the development of more standardised methodologies and best practices for the evaluation of sign language technology.

Acknowledgments

We want to express our thanks to the deaf researchers that joined the feedback session for their insights. We gratefully acknowledge financial support from the Netherlands Organisation for Innovation in Healthcare (ZonMw, grant number 10430042010027) and the European Research Council (ERC, grant number 680220).

References

Bouillon, P., David, B., Strasly, I., and Spechbach, H. (2021). A speech translation system for medical dialogue in sign language—Questionnaire on user perspective of videos and the use of Avatar Technology. In *Proceedings of the 3rd Swiss Conference on Barrier-free Communication (BfC 2020)*, pages 46–54.

David, B. V. C. and Bouillon, P. (2018). Prototype of Automatic Translation to the Sign Language of French-speaking Belgium. Evaluation by the Deaf Community. *Modelling, Measurement and Control C*, 79(4):162–167.

Ebling, S. and Glauert, J. (2016). Building a Swiss German Sign Language avatar with JASigning and evaluating it among the Deaf community. *Universal Access in the Information Society*, 15(4):577–587.

Gibet, S., Courty, N., Duarte, K., and Naour, T. L. (2011). The SignCom system for data-driven animation of interactive virtual signers: Methodology and evaluation. *ACM Transactions on Interactive Intelligent Systems (TiiS)*, 1(1):1–23.

Huenerfauth, M. (2006). *Generating American Sign Language classifier predicates for English-to-ASL machine translation.* PhD thesis, University of Pennsylvania.

Kacorri, H., Huenerfauth, M., Ebling, S., Patel, K., and Willard, M. (2015). Demographic and experiential factors influencing acceptance of sign language animation by deaf users. In *Proceedings of the 17th International ACM SIGACCESS Conference on Computers & Accessibility*, pages 147–154.

Kennaway, R., Glauert, J., and Zwitserlood, I. (2007). Providing signed content on the internet by synthesized animation. *ACM Transactions on Computer-Human Interaction*, 14(3):1–29.

Miller, G. A. (1956). The magical number seven, plus or minus two: Some limits on our capacity for processing information. *Psychological review*, 63:81–97.

Quandt, L. C., Willis, A., Schwenk, M., Weeks, K., and Ferster, R. (2021). Attitudes toward signing human avatars vary depending on hearing status, age of signed language exposure, and avatar type. Manuscript archived at PsyArXiv, June 25, doi:10.31234/osf.io/g2wuc.

Roelofsen, F., Esselink, L., Mende-Gillings, S., and Smeijers, A. (2021). Sign language translation in a healthcare setting. In *Translation and Interpreting Technology*.

Schnepp, J., Wolfe, R., Shiver, B., McDonald, J., and Toro, J. (2011). SignQUOTE: A remote testing facility for eliciting signed qualitative feedback. In *Second International Workshop on Sign Language Translation and Avatar Technology (SLTAT)-2011*.

Smith, R. G. and Nolan, B. (2016). Emotional facial expressions in synthesised sign language avatars: a manual evaluation. *Universal Access in the Information Society*, 15(4):567–576.

Frozen Pretrained Transformers for Neural Sign Language Translation

Mathieu De Coster mathieu.decoster@ugent.be
IDLab-AIRO - Ghent University - imec, Technologiepark-Zwijnaarde 126, Ghent, Belgium

Karel D'Oosterlinck karel.doosterlinck@ugent.be
Marija Pizurica marija.pizurica@ugent.be
Paloma Rabaey paloma.rabaey@ugent.be
Severine Verlinden severine.verlinden@ugent.be
Ghent University, Jozef Plateaustraat 22, Ghent, Belgium

Mieke Van Herreweghe mieke.vanherreweghe@ugent.be
Ghent University, Blandijnberg 2, Ghent, Belgium

Joni Dambre joni.dambre@ugent.be
IDLab-AIRO - Ghent University - imec, Technologiepark-Zwijnaarde 126, Ghent, Belgium

Abstract

One of the major challenges in sign language translation from a sign language to a spoken language is the lack of parallel corpora. Recent works have achieved promising results on the RWTH-PHOENIX-Weather 2014T dataset, which consists of over eight thousand parallel sentences between German sign language and German. However, from the perspective of neural machine translation, this is still a tiny dataset. To improve the performance of models trained on small datasets, transfer learning can be used. While this has been previously applied in sign language translation for feature extraction, to the best of our knowledge, pretrained language models have not yet been investigated. We use pretrained BERT-base and mBART-50 models to initialize our sign language video to spoken language text translation model. To mitigate overfitting, we apply the frozen pretrained transformer technique: we freeze the majority of parameters during training. Using a pretrained BERT model, we outperform a baseline trained from scratch by 1 to 2 BLEU-4. Our results show that pretrained language models can be used to improve sign language translation performance and that the self-attention patterns in BERT transfer in zero-shot to the encoder and decoder of sign language translation models.

1 Introduction

Despite recent advancements in the domain of automated sign language translation (SLT), substantial challenges remain. One considerable issue is the lack of labeled data. Deep neural networks are data-hungry and neural machine translation models are no exception. The widely used SLT dataset RWTH-PHOENIX-Weather 2014T (Camgoz et al., 2018) contains only 8,257 parallel sentences. As a comparison: for translation between spoken languages, 6,000 parallel sentences is considered a "tiny" amount (Gu et al., 2018).

In this work, we investigate how transfer learning can be used to improve the generalization of *video-to-text* SLT models in the absence of large datasets. We integrate pretrained language models such as BERT (Devlin et al., 2019) into our translation models, evaluating translation performance with BERT2RND and BERT2BERT models (Rothe et al., 2020). We also use mBART-50 (Tang et al., 2020), which has been trained on corpora of 50 languages, including German, as our goal is to translate from German sign language (DGS) to German.

These pretrained models are prohibitively large for currently available SLT datasets. The base version of BERT, for example, consists of 12 layers compared to 3 layers in the encoder of the translation model of Camgoz et al. (2020). Therefore, we perform aggressive layer pruning and parameter freezing in the pretrained models.

We use the RWTH-PHOENIX-Weather 2014T dataset for which both gloss and text annotations are available. We consider joint continuous sign language recognition (CSLR) and SLT, or Sign2(Gloss+Text), as it is called by Camgoz et al. (2020). We compare several combinations of pretrained transformers and transformers trained from scratch in terms of scores (WER for CSLR and BLEU-4 for SLT) and number of trainable parameters.

Our results show that the BERT based models (BERT2RND, BERT2BERT) perform best. These models allow us to outperform the baseline, i.e., transformers trained from scratch. Due to overfitting, the large mBART-50 model results in significantly worse performance than the baseline. This warrants further investigation in the incorporation of existing language models. We discuss possible options for future work in Section 6.

The source code of this research project is available at `https://github.com/m-decoster/fpt4slt`.

2 Neural Sign Language Translation

Several SLT systems have been proposed in the past, including rule-based systems (Zhao et al., 2000) and statistical methods (Bungeroth and Ney, 2004). We focus specifically on translation from a sign language to a spoken language. To perform this translation, the sign language first needs to be converted into a written or computational form. Various notation systems exist, such as glosses and HamNoSys (Prillwitz, 1989).

Bungeroth and Ney (2004) focus on Text2Gloss and Gloss2Text translation. Recent advancements in deep learning and computer vision now allow for Sign2Text translation, but this requires sizable corpora. Several large datasets exist for sign language *recognition* tasks, in which the goal is to classify glosses from sign language video, e.g., MS-ASL (Vaezi Joze and Koller, 2019), WLASL (Li et al., 2020) and AUTSL (Sincan and Keles, 2020). RWTH-PHOENIX-Weather 2014T is a large public dataset for sign language *translation* (Camgoz et al., 2018). Along with it, a neural SLT model is formalized and introduced: a recurrent encoder-decoder with Luong attention (Luong et al., 2015). This Sign2Gloss2Text model achieves a BLEU-4 score of 18.13 on the test set.

In a follow-up work, the recurrent architecture is replaced by transformers (Camgoz et al., 2020). The authors present a new study showing improvements in BLEU-4 scores for Gloss2Text and Sign2Text translation. By jointly performing CSLR and SLT, they increase the BLEU-4 test score to 21.32.

Yin and Read (2020) further improve the performance of sign language transformers by using multiple cues (face, hand, full frame and pose information, rather than only full frame information) for CSLR and performing Sign2Gloss2Text translation. They achieve a BLEU-4 test score of 24 (25.40 using an ensemble of 5 models). These improvements are related to feature extraction rather than network architecture, whereas we aim to improve the translation model by creating a more powerful encoder-decoder model (an orthogonal approach).

3 Transfer Learning and Frozen Pretrained Transformers

Transfer learning from high-resource to low-resource language pairs can result in better translation performance for low-resource language pairs (Zoph et al., 2016). Pretraining with huge monolingual corpora can also improve performance of downstream tasks such as sentiment classification and question answering (Devlin et al., 2019). Pretrained models such as BERT can also be adapted as encoders or decoders in a machine translation model to improve translation performance (Rothe et al., 2020).

Transfer learning between different sign languages has previously been used to improve model performance in sign language recognition (Pigou et al., 2017; Albanie et al., 2020). The use of a continuous sign language recognition model as feature extractor for SLT, as performed by Camgoz et al. (2020), is also a form of transfer learning. To the best of our knowledge, so far no one has leveraged transfer learning of encoders and decoders (rather than feature extractors) for SLT from signed to spoken languages.

Lu et al. (2021) show that pretrained language models can replace transformers trained from scratch for downstream tasks, even if those downstream tasks are not related to natural language processing (NLP). This is contrary to earlier research, where language models were used in a parameter-efficient transfer learning set-up from one NLP task to another (Houlsby et al., 2019). Self-attention and feedforward layers are frozen and only the layer normalization parameters are fine-tuned. These are, for large language models, only a tiny fraction of the parameters (often less than 1%). As a result, these models, called Frozen Pretrained Transformers (FPTs), are more robust against overfitting. We combine the approaches of Rothe et al. (2020) and Lu et al. (2021) for SLT: we aim to leverage pretrained language models, while freezing the majority of the parameters to avoid overfitting on our extremely small dataset.

4 Methodology

We use the following experimental set-up. First, we reproduce the baseline of Camgoz et al. (2020) using the code base provided by the authors[1]. Then, we lay out several experiments with different models with either an FPT encoder or FPT encoder and decoder. We compare several degrees of fine-tuning, ranging from only layer normalization to everything except the self-attention layers. Due to computational constraints, we use a sequential approach for hyperparameter tuning. However, we tune two correlated hyperparameters together: the number of layers and degree of fine-tuning.

4.1 Sign Language Translation

Our SLT approach follows that of Camgoz et al. (2020). We use a transformer encoder-decoder model with 3 layers and 8 attention heads as a baseline. We use the same features, which were obtained from a model trained on CSLR (Koller et al., 2019). Camgoz et al. (2020) report BLEU-4 scores of 22.38 and 21.32 on the development and test set of RWTH-PHOENIX-Weather 2014T, respectively. These scores are obtained for loss weights $\lambda_R = 10$ and $\lambda_T = 1$. Our reproduction using the code base provided by the authors yields 20.18 and 19.86. The difference is possibly due to a different random seed, resulting in a less than optimal weight initialization in our case. From communication with the authors, we learned that they reported the best result out of ten runs with different random seeds. We select only a single seed and report all of our results using the resulting random initialization.

4.2 Frozen Pretrained Transformers

We run three experiments. We first aim to improve CSLR and SLT performance by integrating an FPT (BERT) in the encoder of the Sign2(Gloss+Text) model. The decoder is trained from scratch. We name this method BERT2RND, according to the nomenclature of Rothe et al. (2020). Secondly, we evaluate a BERT2BERT model, where a cross-attention module is added to the BERT model integrated in the decoder; this module is trained from scratch. Finally, we

[1] `https://github.com/neccam/slt`

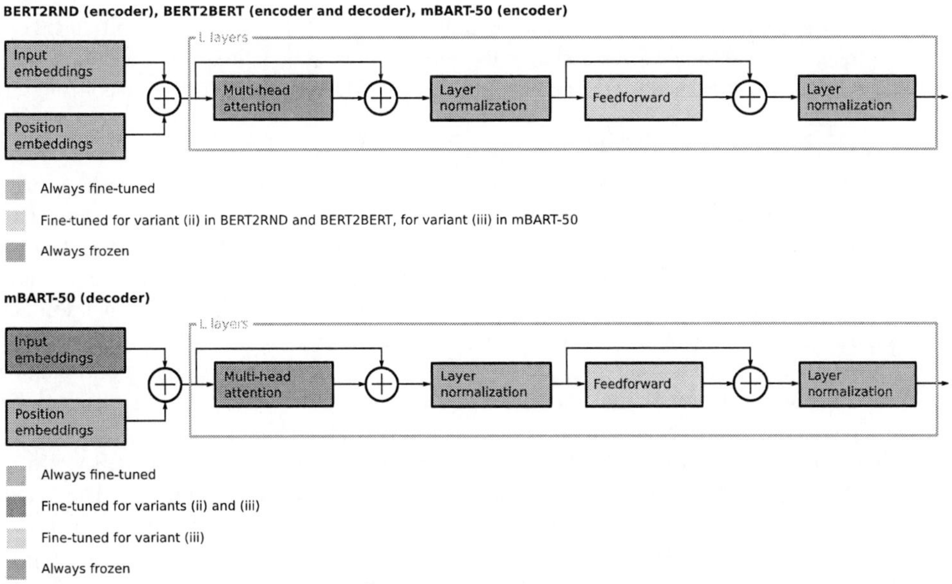

Figure 1: Model variants and the degrees of freezing. BERT2RND only has a pretrained encoder, while for BERT2BERT and mBART-50 both the encoder and decoder are pretrained.

investigate whether integrating a language model pretrained on the target language (German) improves the quality of translations (measured in BLEU-4 scores). We use mBART-50 to initialize both the encoder and decoder. We freeze the pretrained cross-attention module in the decoder, but add a randomly initialized linear layer to transform the encoder outputs such that they better align with the pretrained cross-attention patterns. The German target sentences are tokenized using the mBART-50 tokenizer so that we are able to reuse the token embeddings in the decoder. By default, we freeze the mBART-50 token embeddings as they contain over 250 thousand elements. However, we investigate the impact of freezing and fine-tuning them.

We wish to minimize the amount of trainable parameters to mitigate overfitting. We compare different degrees of fine-tuning (ordered by increasing number of trainable parameters). We name these the "model variants". For BERT2RND and BERT2BERT there are two variants:

(i) fine-tune layer normalization parameters, positional embeddings, sign embeddings and decoder token embeddings,

(ii) fine-tune all of the above and feedforward layers.

For mBART-50 there is an additional variant, because the token embeddings in the decoder are not fine-tuned by default:

(i) fine-tune layer normalization parameters, positional embeddings and sign embeddings only,

(ii) fine-tune all of the above and token embeddings,

(iii) fine-tune all of the above and feedforward layers.

A schematic overview of which layers are frozen and which are not is shown in Figure 1.

For every model, we train a linear input layer for which the weights are initialized orthogonally in the encoder and as Gaussian in the decoder - based on findings by Lu et al. (2021). No such input layer is trained for the decoder in BERT2RND as the decoder is trained from scratch.

4.3 Hyperparameter Tuning

We tune several hyperparameters, including the learning rate, number of layers, loss weights, decoding beam size and beam alpha. Note that we aim to optimize the translation score (BLEU-4) rather than the continuous sign language recognition score (WER). All hyperparameter tuning and model selection is therefore performed based on the BLEU-4 score. We first tune the learning rate per model architecture on a model with 3 layers in both encoder and decoder (the same as the baseline model). We then perform all further tuning and experiments with the learning rate that yields the highest development set BLEU-4 score. Ideally, one would tune the learning rate together with the other hyperparameters (number of layers, loss weights), but the computational cost prohibits this for our experiments. The optimal learning rates obtained for each model are 3e$-$4 for BERT2RND, 1e$-$4 for BERT2BERT and 1e$-$3 for mBART-50.

We then perform simple layer pruning to reduce the model complexity. The amount of layers that we keep is a hyperparameter n (between 1 and the number of layers in the pretrained transformer) that is tuned to maximize the development set BLEU-4 score. When pruning, we always keep the first n layers, and replace deeper ones by identity functions. The number of layers n is tuned for all model variants as we hypothesize that freezing more parameters per layer allows for deeper networks. Because of computational constraints, we cannot check all values of n for all models. Because deeper models rapidly start overfitting, we choose $n = 1, 2, 3, 6, 12$ (12 being the original number of layers in BERT-base and mBART-50). For BERT2RND, the decoder is kept as it is in the original implementation: a 3 layer transformer trained from scratch.

We select the optimal number of layers per experiment and tune the loss weight $\lambda_R = 1, 5, 10$, as Camgoz et al. (2020) show that this can have a large impact on the translation score.

After training of each experiment, the best beam size and alpha are found by tuning for both WER and BLEU-4 on the development set. The results are reported on the development set and test set using these parameters.

All models are optimized with a batch size of 32, with the Adam optimizer (Kingma and Ba, 2015). The optimizer parameters are set to $\beta = (0.9, 0.998)$ and the weight decay to 1e$-$3, as per Camgoz et al. (2020). We also apply a similar learning rate scheduling approach: we decrease the learning rate with a factor 0.7 whenever the development set BLEU-4 score has not increased for 800 iterations. We stop training when the learning rate is smaller than 1e$-$7.

5 Results

We find an optimal number of layers and loss weights for the different models based on the development set BLEU-4 score. We discuss the amount of trainable parameters for the optimal models found for each variant, while at the same time listing the development set score for the optimal models. We finally compare the development set and test set results with the baseline.

5.1 Optimal Number of Layers

We find that for all three model architectures, the optimal number of layers is low. This is as expected due to the small dataset size. For BERT2RND, the difference in performance between freezing approaches is small for a low layer count. For larger layer counts, fine-tuning only the layer normalization parameters (model variant (i)) yields better performance, because this model overfits less than the others. For BERT2BERT, fine-tuning the feedforward layers consistently results in better performance. The gap between the model variants is larger than for

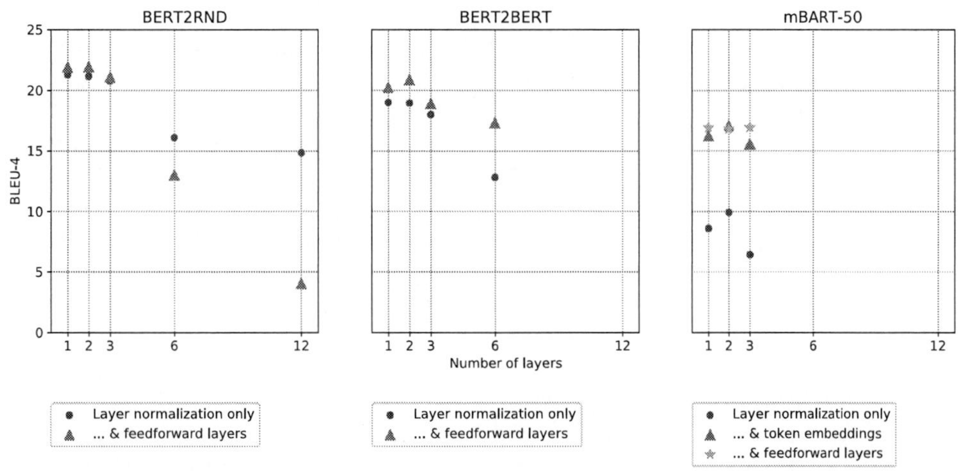

Figure 2: BLEU-4 scores for different model sizes of the three architectures, for $\lambda_R = \lambda_T = 1$. The models reach the highest BLEU-4 scores for 1, 2 or 3 layers. The missing values for BERT2BERT with 12 layers and for mBART-50 with 6 and 12 layers are due to VRAM constraints.

Table 1: The number of trainable parameters of different models and their best obtained development set BLEU-4 score. The best result is indicated in bold.

Model	Variant	Layers	Trainable parameters	BLEU-4
Transformer	N/A	3	38,878,270	20.18
BERT2RND	(i)	1	30,292,542	21.28
	(ii)	2	39,740,478	**22.47**
BERT2BERT	(i)	2	34,195,518	20.87
	(ii)	2	53,085,246	21.26
mBART-50	(i)	2	7,180,606	10.64
	(ii)	2	263,235,902	17.06
	(iii)	3	313,608,510	16.92

BERT2RND. We assume that the decoder benefits more from having more degrees of freedom than the encoder. The mBART-50 model underfits when the token embeddings are not fine-tuned: model variant (i) only achieves a maximum BLEU-4 score of 9.95 for 2 layers. The scores are consistently lower than for BERT2RND and BERT2BERT. Fine-tuning the decoder token embeddings is clearly required. However, even then we are unable to achieve baseline performance with mBART-50. An overview of the results is shown in Figure 2.

5.2 Amount of Trainable Parameters

We list the number of trainable parameters for every model variant in Table 1. We only consider the optimal number of layers (see Figure 2). The baseline count is 39 million. While several of our FPT models have more trainable parameters (including our best model with 40 million), we are able to match the baseline performance using a 1-layer BERT2RND model where only the layer normalization parameters are fine-tuned (30 million parameters). In this model, the self-attention encoder only has 600 thousand trainable parameters (1 layer), compared to 9 million when training a 3-layer encoder from scratch.

Table 2: Comparison of WER and BLEU-4 scores for the baseline and our best FPT models. The best results are indicated in bold.

Model	Development		Test	
	WER ↓	BLEU-4 ↑	WER ↓	BLEU-4 ↑
Transformer (Camgoz et al., 2020)	**24.98**	22.38	**26.16**	21.32
Transformer (reproduced)	30.48	20.18	29.96	19.86
BERT2RND (ii, 2 layers, $\lambda_R = 5$)	36.59	**22.47**	35.76	**22.25**
BERT2BERT (ii, 2 layers, $\lambda_R = 10$)	40.99	21.26	39.99	21.16
mBART-50 (ii, 2 layers, $\lambda_R = 1$)	40.25	17.06	39.43	16.64

5.3 Comparison with the Baseline

We compare the best results for each model architecture with the best results reported by Camgoz et al. (2020). The comparison is shown in Table 2. The best model is the 2-layer BERT2RND model with fine-tuning of feedforward layers (variant (ii)). With a test BLEU-4 score of 22.25, it outperforms the baseline. We see an increase of 0.93 compared to the baseline established by Camgoz et al. (2020) and of 2.39 compared to our reproduction of that model. A 2-layer BERT2BERT model with fine-tuning of feedforward layers outperforms the reproduced baseline by 1.3 BLEU-4, and achieves comparable performance to the model reported in the previous work. For mBART-50, we find that a 2-layer model with frozen attention patterns and feedforward layers achieves 16.64 BLEU-4.

6 Discussion

In this work, we have proposed using FPTs for neural SLT. We have compared several encoder-decoder architectures:

- BERT2RND, where the encoder is an FPT initialized from BERT-base
- BERT2BERT, where both encoder and decoder are FPTs initialized from BERT-base
- mBART-50, where encoder and decoder are FPTs initialized from mBART-50

6.1 Comparison Between Architectures

Out of these architectures, BERT2RND achieves the best results, with a BLEU-4 test score of 22.25 (an increase of 0.93 compared to the baseline established by Camgoz et al. (2020) and of 2.39 compared to our reproduction of that model). The best BERT2BERT model achieves 21.16. When freezing more parameters, we see a larger performance drop than for BERT2RND. Likely, the decoder benefits more from being trained from scratch or fine-tuned.

Contrary to our expectations, using mBART-50 pre-trained on (among others) German text, did not improve the translation quality for SLT with German as the target language. In fact, mBART-50 yields results below the baseline: 16.64 BLEU-4. We observe that fine-tuning the token embeddings is essential: freezing them results in a catastrophic drop in performance. Fine-tuning the cross-attention module to allow better alignment between the sign language encoder representations and spoken language decoder representations could prove useful, but brings with it the risk of overfitting.

6.2 Perspective and Future Work

The use of FPTs in low-resource scenarios such as SLT appears promising. FPTs can be integrated in translation models to improve translation performance. Our experiments show that for comparable performance, FPTs can be slightly shallower than transformers trained from scratch. This could prove useful for reducing the computational cost during inference.

Techniques such as tokenization and (neural) embedding computation of written text have matured more than feature extraction for SLT due to machine translation between spoken languages receiving more research attention than SLT. Furthermore, current state of the art machine translation models are designed first and foremost for translation between spoken languages. Architectural changes may prove beneficial or even necessary to obtain better SLT performance. This is reflected in our results. Modelling sign language (in the encoder) appears to benefit more from pretrained language models than the modelling of spoken languages (in the decoder).

Further research should investigate the use of smaller, bilingual, models as FPTs. Fine-tuning the translation model on written texts concerning the topics present in the SLT data (before training on actual sign language data) may also result in better translations. Finally, another interesting research track is the integration of a translation model as a prior rather than as an FPT (Baziotis et al., 2020).

Next to trying to find better architectures for sign language translation, better feature extraction methods are also being researched. Any advancements in feature extraction for SLT can be combined with architectural improvements such as FPTs to further increase the quality of the translation model.

While SLT models have significantly improved in terms of translation metrics over the past few years, there still remains a large gap to bridge before they can be applied in real-world settings. In particular, these metrics, such as BLEU scores, do not always match well with the perceived quality of the translations by human evaluators (Callison-Burch et al., 2006). For this reason, future work will focus on identifying the main shortcomings that need to be addressed in SLT in order to achieve its performance acceptable for Deaf and Hard of Hearing (DHH) communities. This question needs to be addressed from, both, a technical and a linguistic perspective, and in close collaboration with the end users of potential SLT applications. Co-creation with DHH community members is therefore key.

7 Conclusion

We have presented and compared three different approaches to using pretrained language models for a Sign2(Gloss+Text) SLT task: BERT2RND, BERT2BERT and mBART-50. We outperform the baseline, which is a transformer trained from scratch, by replacing the encoder with the first 2 layers of BERT-base. We freeze the attention patterns and show that the patterns learned during the training of the BERT model transfer in zero-shot to SLT. The decoder can also be initialized using a pretrained language model, but we obtain better results if the decoder is trained from scratch. We attempt to integrate mBART-50, a multi-lingual translation model, hoping to obtain translations of a higher quality due to this model having been pretrained on German texts. However, we are unable to reach baseline performance with mBART-50. Further research should investigate whether smaller translation models obtain better performance, or whether language models can be used as priors to regularize the SLT model. Our best result, a BLEU-4 score of 22.25 on the test set of RWTH-PHOENIX-Weather 2014T, is obtained using a BERT2RND model. The BERT2RND methodology is easy to implement and can be combined with other advances such as improvements in feature extraction.

Acknowledgements

Mathieu De Coster's research is funded by the Research Foundation Flanders (FWO Vlaanderen): file number 77410. This work has been conducted within the SignON project. This project has received funding from the European Union's Horizon 2020 research and innovation programme under grant agreement No 101017255.

References

Albanie, S., Varol, G., Momeni, L., Afouras, T., Chung, J. S., Fox, N., and Zisserman, A. (2020). BSL-1K: Scaling up co-articulated sign language recognition using mouthing cues. In *European Conference on Computer Vision*, pages 35–53. Springer.

Baziotis, C., Haddow, B., and Birch, A. (2020). Language model prior for low-resource neural machine translation. In *Proceedings of the 2020 Conference on Empirical Methods in Natural Language Processing (EMNLP)*, pages 7622–7634.

Bungeroth, J. and Ney, H. (2004). Statistical sign language translation. In *Workshop on representation and processing of sign languages, LREC*, volume 4, pages 105–108. Citeseer.

Callison-Burch, C., Osborne, M., and Koehn, P. (2006). Re-evaluating the role of BLEU in machine translation research. In *11th Conference of the European Chapter of the Association for Computational Linguistics*.

Camgoz, N. C., Hadfield, S., Koller, O., Ney, H., and Bowden, R. (2018). Neural sign language translation. In *Proceedings of the IEEE Conference on Computer Vision and Pattern Recognition*, pages 7784–7793.

Camgoz, N. C., Koller, O., Hadfield, S., and Bowden, R. (2020). Sign language transformers: Joint end-to-end sign language recognition and translation. In *Proceedings of the IEEE/CVF Conference on Computer Vision and Pattern Recognition*, pages 10023–10033.

Devlin, J., Chang, M.-W., Lee, K., and Toutanova, K. (2019). BERT: Pre-training of deep bidirectional transformers for language understanding. In *Proceedings of the 2019 Conference of the North American Chapter of the Association for Computational Linguistics: Human Language Technologies, Volume 1 (Long and Short Papers)*, pages 4171–4186, Minneapolis, Minnesota. Association for Computational Linguistics.

Gu, J., Hassan, H., Devlin, J., and Li, V. O. (2018). Universal neural machine translation for extremely low resource languages. In *Proceedings of the 2018 Conference of the North American Chapter of the Association for Computational Linguistics: Human Language Technologies, Volume 1 (Long Papers)*, pages 344–354.

Houlsby, N., Giurgiu, A., Jastrzebski, S., Morrone, B., De Laroussilhe, Q., Gesmundo, A., Attariyan, M., and Gelly, S. (2019). Parameter-efficient transfer learning for NLP. In Chaudhuri, K. and Salakhutdinov, R., editors, *Proceedings of the 36th International Conference on Machine Learning*, volume 97 of *Proceedings of Machine Learning Research*, pages 2790–2799. PMLR.

Kingma, D. P. and Ba, J. (2015). Adam: A method for stochastic optimization. In Bengio, Y. and LeCun, Y., editors, *3rd International Conference on Learning Representations, ICLR 2015, San Diego, CA, USA, May 7-9, 2015, Conference Track Proceedings*.

Koller, O., Camgoz, N. C., Ney, H., and Bowden, R. (2019). Weakly supervised learning with multi-stream CNN-LSTM-HMMs to discover sequential parallelism in sign language videos. *IEEE transactions on pattern analysis and machine intelligence*, 42(9):2306–2320.

Li, D., Rodriguez, C., Yu, X., and Li, H. (2020). Word-level Deep Sign Language Recognition from Video: A New Large-scale Dataset and Methods Comparison. In *Proceedings of the IEEE/CVF Winter Conference on Applications of Computer Vision (WACV)*.

Lu, K., Grover, A., Abbeel, P., and Mordatch, I. (2021). Pretrained transformers as universal computation engines. *arXiv preprint arXiv:2103.05247*.

Luong, M.-T., Pham, H., and Manning, C. D. (2015). Effective approaches to attention-based neural machine translation. In *Proceedings of the 2015 Conference on Empirical Methods in Natural Language Processing*, pages 1412–1421.

Pigou, L., Van Herreweghe, M., and Dambre, J. (2017). Gesture and sign language recognition with temporal residual networks. In *Proceedings of the IEEE International Conference on Computer Vision Workshops*, pages 3086–3093.

Prillwitz, S. (1989). *HamNoSys: Version 2.0; Hamburg notation system for sign languages; an introductory guide*. Signum-Verlag.

Rothe, S., Narayan, S., and Severyn, A. (2020). Leveraging pre-trained checkpoints for sequence generation tasks. *Transactions of the Association for Computational Linguistics*, 8:264–280.

Sincan, O. M. and Keles, H. Y. (2020). AUTSL: A Large Scale Multi-Modal Turkish Sign Language Dataset and Baseline Methods. *IEEE Access*, 8:181340–181355.

Tang, Y., Tran, C., Li, X., Chen, P.-J., Goyal, N., Chaudhary, V., Gu, J., and Fan, A. (2020). Multilingual translation with extensible multilingual pretraining and finetuning. *arXiv preprint arXiv:2008.00401*.

Vaezi Joze, H. and Koller, O. (2019). MS-ASL: A large-scale data set and benchmark for understanding American Sign Language. In *The British Machine Vision Conference (BMVC)*.

Yin, K. and Read, J. (2020). Better sign language translation with STMC-transformer. In *Proceedings of the 28th International Conference on Computational Linguistics*, pages 5975–5989.

Zhao, L., Kipper, K., Schuler, W., Vogler, C., Badler, N., and Palmer, M. (2000). A machine translation system from English to American Sign Language. In *Conference of the Association for Machine Translation in the Americas*, pages 54–67. Springer.

Zoph, B., Yuret, D., May, J., and Knight, K. (2016). Transfer learning for low-resource neural machine translation. In *Proceedings of the 2016 Conference on Empirical Methods in Natural Language Processing*, pages 1568–1575, Austin, Texas. Association for Computational Linguistics.

Defining meaningful units. Challenges in sign segmentation and segment-meaning mapping

Mirella De Sisto m.desisto@tilburguniversity.edu
Dimitar Shterionov d.shterionov@tilburguniversity.edu
Department of Cognitive Science and Artificial Intelligence, Tilburg University, Netherlands

Irene Murtagh irene.murtagh@tudublin.ie
Department of Informatics, Technological University Dublin, Ireland

Myriam Vermeerbergen myriam.vermeerbergen@kuleuven.be
Faculty of Arts, KU Leuven, Belgium

Lorraine Leeson leesonl@tcd.ie
Centre for Deaf Studies, Trinity College Dublin, Ireland

Abstract

This paper addresses the tasks of sign segmentation and segment-meaning mapping in the context of sign language (SL) recognition. It aims to give an overview of the linguistic properties of SL, such as coarticulation and simultaneity, which make these tasks complex. A better understanding of SL structure is the necessary ground for the design and development of SL recognition and segmentation methodologies, which are fundamental for machine translation of these languages. Based on this preliminary exploration, a proposal for mapping segments to meaning in the form of an agglomerate of lexical and non-lexical information is introduced.

1 Introduction

The first steps for a machine translation (MT) pipeline which targets signed languages are: 1) defining a way to transcribe the sign stream that exhaustively describes all articulated features; 2) subdividing the transcriptions into units and 3) connecting these units to meaning.[1]

In this work, we employ Sign_A (Murtagh, 2019) to address the first step. Sign_A provides a detailed description of the (computational) phonological parameters that are essential to articulate the various phonemes, morphemes and lexemes of a SL utterance. In Murtagh (2019), Sign_A transcriptions are combined with Role and Reference Grammar (RRG), a form of syntactic representation that considers semantic and communicative functions (Valin, 1993), i.e. addressing the third step; however, Sign_A is not automatically connected to RRG currently. So, how to connect Sign_A transcriptions to meaning is an open question at this stage; it largely depends on defining meaningful units that can be linked with meaning, i.e. step 2.

In order to know what kind (or format) of meaning needs to be mapped to Sign_A (and vice-versa) and how, we need to know how the utterance is subdivided into parts. For example, if we consider a written utterance, the text is normally subdivided into tokens (words, punctuation

[1]While current deep learning methods allow for efficient end-to-end approaches, the complexity of SLs and the lack of annotated data makes the use of such methods infeasible.

marks, etc.), via tokenization; tokens can then be used in meaning mapping operations, such as, e.g. Part of Speech tagging, MT, and others, to derive knowledge. In signed languages, as well, it is necessary to define how to split the sign stream. Moryossef (2021)[2], and Yin et al. (2021) discuss the problems related to sign tokenization. Tokenization, as we know it for spoken languages, cannot be easily applied to signed languages; some properties of these types of languages, such as simultaneity and coarticulation, make the identification of single word-like units in the signed stream not a viable task. Moryossef (2021) proposes to tackle this issue through sign segmentation. Nevertheless, the difficulty in defining segment boundaries makes this approach problematic as well. Some studies have explored this form of subdividing a signed utterance but reliable and constant boundary predictors have still to be found (see Ormel and Crasborn (2012); Yin et al. (2021) for details).

In this paper we first give an overview of the properties of SLs that make stream segmentation problematic. Next, we introduce a work-in-progress possible approach for mapping sign transcriptions (in Sign_A) to meaning.

2 Why is segmentation difficult?

Stokoe (1960) described signs as being much more simultaneously organised than words:"Signs are not holistic units, but are made up of specific formational units: hand configuration, movement, and location." Zeshan (2007) proposed that signs in SL are situated at an equivalent level of organisation as words in spoken language. Following Brennan (1992), Leeson and Saeed (2012) identify signs in SL as equivalent to words in spoken language in terms of grammatical role. However, not every sign carries the same type of meaning that can make it comparable to words in spoken languages. A distinction can be made between established signs — also defined as Fully Lexical Signs, (Johnston, 2016), or Lexemes (Johnston and Schembri, 1999) — and productive lexicon (Vermeerbergen and Van Herreweghe, 2018) — Partly-Lexical Signs (Johnston, 2016). Established signs have a conventionalised form and meaning that are consistent across contexts (Vermeerbergen and Van Herreweghe, 2018). The meaning to which these lexemes are strongly associated is specific (Johnston and Schembri, 1999). Since they have a clear citation form (Johnston and Schembri, 1999), they can also be easily identified within a continuous sign stream. Productive signs, instead, are context-dependent; the possibility of creating new not lexicalised signs is enormous and this practice is very productive in signed languages (see Johnston and Schembri (1999); Belissen (2020). Using language components for creating new forms is a property common to both signed and spoken languages; however, the componentiality of signs allows signers to use innovative forms more frequently than it could possibly happen in spoken languages. This productivity can constitute a problem for sign segmentation, since new signs do not have a pre-defined form.

The most salient element in identifying a sign appears to be hand movement; however, we find discordant opinions about using it for identifying a segment, since it is always realised in combination with other elements (Johnston and Schembri, 1999; Khan, 2014). Nevertheless, hand movement can be used for identification of established signs; but it cannot account for productive signs and the extra information provided by other articulators.

Another trait of the sign that makes it different from the word in spoken languages is the difficulty in identifying its edges in a sign stream. All speakers of one language are able to easily subdivide an utterance into words; moreover, they will subdivide the same utterance in the same way, by following the same phonetic and phonological properties (Brentari, 2006). The same cannot be easily said for SL segmentation: studies on segmentation made by humans show variability and multiplicity of cues at play, and the difficulty in identifying the dominant cues; there is no agreement among researchers about whether signers (and non-signers) can

[2] `https://www.youtube.com/watch?v=ayDKJ6_nKeY`

provide the same segmentation (Brentari, 2006; Fenlon, 2010; Brentari et al., 2011) or whether they have discordant intuitions (Hanke et al., 2012; Khan, 2014; Gabarró-López and Meurant, 2014). In addition, the possibility for signers to identify cues by using lexical and grammatical knowledge needs to be considered as well (Fenlon, 2010).

Various technical approaches to sign segmentation have been proposed, such as based on minimum hand velocity and large directional variation, combining velocity with trajectory curvature or temporal localisation, minimal pairs distinction (Khan, 2014), and transitional movements removal (Hanke et al., 2012). A flaw of these approaches is that they do not specify what kind of units are considered from a linguistic point of view, or simply refer to a generic 'word'.

Perceptual studies generally focus on identifying boundaries of parts of the utterance which are bigger than words, such as sentences or prosodic groups (Ormel and Crasborn, 2012; Gabarró-López and Meurant, 2014). By looking at the prosodic structure (Selkirk, 1984; Nespor and Vogel, 1986) these studies follow the assumption that prosodic cues can contribute to identifying syntactic structure.[3] Prosodic cues can be part of manual and nonmanual articulators; usually, the latter add semantic information to the former (Ormel and Crasborn, 2012). Nonmanual articulators have been considered for prosodic boundaries detection: either by being considered as markers of phrase edges or as domain markers based on their duration (Ormel and Crasborn, 2012). Boundary markers occur at phrase boundaries, they can be pause, eye blinks, head nods, reduplication, hand hold, and final lengthening; domain markers are spread across signs within a phrase, they can be facial, head and body movements (see Nespor and Sandler (1999); Brentari and Crossley (2002); Ormel and Crasborn (2012). Eye blinks are among the most frequently mentioned boundary markers, often in combination with other cues; however, if considered in isolation they are not a consistent boundary cue (Ormel and Crasborn, 2012). Several and combined nonmanual cues can function as boundary markers and there seems to be no evidence for one cue or a specific combination to play a dominant role (Nespor and Sandler, 1999; Fenlon, 2010; Ormel and Crasborn, 2012; Gabarró-López and Meurant, 2014).

Coarticulation appears to be the major obstacle to a straightforward boundary detection.[4] There are more forms of coarticulation, such as: hold deletion, metathesis, assimilation and movement epenthesis (Khan, 2014). Simultaneity of manual and nonmanual articulators might also constitute a problem to segmentation; different types of information are communicated at the same time, hence they cannot be easily subdivided. Simultaneity can also cause overlapping of complex structures like sentences; in which case differentiating and splitting the two sentence layers can be challenging (Crasborn, 2007). Vermeerbergen et al. (2007) define three types of simultaneity, namely manual simultaneity, manual-oral simultaneity and simultaneous use of other (manual and nonmanual) articulators.

3 Representations of signs

To date, there is no tradition of writing signed languages (Frishberg et al., 2012). Several sign notation systems have been developed, but none of them evolved into being widely accepted and used. In the 1960s Stokoe (1960) defined a set of symbols to notate the components of each sign of American Sign Language (mostly intended for dictionary entries). Later, in the 1970s, Valerie Sutton introduced a writing system for SL based on a dance notation, called

[3] As in spoken languages, syntactic and prosodic constituents are non-isomorphic (Nespor and Vogel, 1986); however, intonation and rhythm can provide useful information for sentence segmentation (Ormel and Crasborn, 2012).

[4] However, checking whether a coarticulation process only occurs within a prosodic domain and not across boundaries can be evidence of the existence of these boundaries and might be used for linguistic segmentation (in this respect, see Nespor and Sandler (1999). A limit to this approach is the optionality of coarticulation phenomena generally, which might prevent them from being reliable cues.

SignWriting.[5] It is made up of schematized iconic symbols for the hands, face and body, with additional notations for location and direction and intents to capture gestural behaviour in the flow of performance. More recently, the Hamburg Notation System (HamNoSys) was created to transcribe signs from many different signed languages (Prillwitz, 1989). It is a very detailed transcription system that was developed in conjunction with a standard computer font, mainly to be used for linguistic analysis. The notation of signs or a SL using any of these notation/writing systems results in a (more or less detailed) representation of the signs for their physical forms.

Representing the meaning of signs is most commonly done by using glosses consisting of words drawn from the spoken language of the surrounding community or in books and articles of the language of publication. Glosses are most often used for representing the manual signs. Typically, established signs are represented by capital letters glosses, and productive signs with several words. The use of glosses to annotate natural signed discourse is not without difficulty nor risk (Vermeerbergen, 2006; Frishberg et al., 2012). For example, using words from a spoken language to represent the meaning of a sign can lead to an inappropriate semantic of grammatical analysis of that sign. Another important problem is that there is no standardized way of glossing, and that gloss annotations differ between - and sometimes even within - corpora.

The Sign_A framework (Murtagh, 2019) was developed in the pursuit of defining a lexicon architecture that is sufficiently robust in nature to accommodate SL. The "A" in Sign_A refers to Articulatory Structure Level. This level of lexical meaning aims to represent the essential (computational) phonological parameters of an object as defined by the lexical item. These parameters will be used to account for various linguistic phenomena pertaining to manual and non-manual features.

RRG can be described as a structural functionalist theory of grammar and a functional model of language. RRG is a monostratal theory positing only one level of syntactic representation, the actual form of the sentence. Therefore, there is only one syntactic representation for a sentence. This representation corresponds to the actual form of the sentence. Leveraging RRG in combination with Sign_A allows for the development of a lexicon architecture capable of accommodating SL in computational linguistic terms.

While our work focuses on Sign_A as a representation of a signed message, we acknowledge that the proposed method can be applied, after some adaptation, to signed messages represented in other notations.

4 Provisional proposal

Since nonmanual articulators add semantic information to manual articulators (Ormel and Crasborn, 2012), it might be possible to use the manual articulators as bases for a segment, i.e. as a 'root' of an environment bigger than a word. We propose to map the Sign_A transcription to an 'enriched glosses' structure, where the lexical entry is enriched with the surrounding features conveying meaning (so having blocks like noun phrases or verb phrases). These enriched glosses can be compatible with and resemble glosses used for spoken languages (see The Leipzig Glossing Rule[6]). Meaning can be implemented with RRG specifications or morphological information. These glosses (enriched with RRG) from one signed or spoken language could then be reconverted in either a spoken or a SL output through an MT approach (see, for instance, Zhou et al. (2020). Using enriched glosses might prevent information loss that takes place when glosses for signed languages are used (Stokoe, 1980; Yin et al., 2021). Glosses for signed languages are mostly used to transcribe lexemes only, while enriched glosses would include other pieces of information; for instance, the morphological suffixation that modifies the lexeme. With this approach, SL glosses would be similar to those of agglutinative lan-

[5]www.signwriting.org

[6]www.eva.mpg.de/lingua/pdf/Glossing-Rules.pdf

guages (e.g. Turkish), which express grammatical information in an agglomerate of sub-units (i.e. many morphemes attach to one root); of course, a significant distinction remains: agglutinative languages units behave in a linear way like other spoken languages (i.e. one morpheme is attached next to the other, in a flat structure), while signs have simultaneous components.

Enriched glosses aim to address the structural complexity of these languages and to provide an exhaustive form of denoting meaning. Being able to account for any meaningful element of the sign stream is a fundamental aspect for the preservation of the message, and for its efficient translation.

5 Conclusion

In this paper we discussed the challenges to sign segmentation and to segment-meaning mapping. After an overview of the SL properties which need to be considered when addressing segmentation, we outlined a proposal, employing the Sign_A formalism, for connecting segments to meaning into an agglomerate of lexical and non-lexical information.

References

Belissen, V. (2020). *From Sign Recognition to Automatic Sign Language Understanding: Addressing the Non-Conventionalized Units.* PhD thesis, Paris-Saclay University.

Brennan, M. (1992). The visual world of BSL: An introduction. In Brien, D., editor, *Dictionary of British Sign Language/English*, pages 1–133. London: Faber and Faber.

Brentari, D. (2006). Effects of language modality on word segmentation: An experimental study of phonological factors in a sign language. In Goldstein, L., Whalen, D. H., and Best, C. T., editors, *Phonology and Phonetics [PP].* Mouton de Gruyter, Berlin, New York.

Brentari, D. and Crossley, L. (2002). Prosody on the hands and face: Evidence from American Sign Language. *Sign Language & Linguistics*, 5(2):105–130.

Brentari, D., González, C., Seidl, A., and Wilbur, R. (2011). Sensitivity to Visual Prosodic Cues in Signers and Nonsigners. *Language and Speech*, 54(1):49–72.

Crasborn, O. A. (2007). How to recognise a sentence when you see one. *Sign Language & Linguistics*, 10(2):103–111.

Fenlon, J. J. (2010). *Seeing sentence boundaries: the production and perception of visual markers signalling boundaries in signed languages.* PhD thesis, University College London.

Frishberg, N., Hoiting, N., and Slobin, D. I. (2012). *Transcription*, pages 1045–1075. De Gruyter Mouton.

Gabarró-López, S. and Meurant, L. (2014). When nonmanuals meet semantics and syntax: a practical guide for the segmentation of sign language discourse. In *6th Workshop on the Representation and Processing of Sign Languages: Beyond the Manual Channel*, Reykjavik, Iceland.

Hanke, T., Matthes, S., Regen, A., and Worseck, S. (2012). Where Does a Sign Start and End? Segmentation of Continuous Signing. In *5th Workshop on the Representation and Processing of Sign Languages: Interactions between Corpus and Lexicon (LREC 2012)*, page 6.

Johnston, T. (2016). *Auslan Corpus Annotation Guidelines.* Centre for Language Sciences, Department of Linguistics, Macquarie University.

Johnston, T. and Schembri, A. C. (1999). On Defining Lexeme in a Signed Language. *Sign Language & Linguistics*, 2(2):115–185.

Khan, S. (2014). *Segmentation of continuous sign language*. PhD thesis, Massey University.

Leeson, L. and Saeed, J. (2012). *Irish Sign Language*. Edinburgh, UK: Edinburgh University Press.

Moryossef, A. (2021). Including signed languages in natural language processing. Talk at ETH.

Murtagh, I. E. (2019). *A Linguistically Motivated Computational Framework for Irish Sign Language*. PhD thesis, Trinity College Dublin.School of Linguistic Speech and Comm Sci.

Nespor, M. and Sandler, W. (1999). Prosody in Israeli Sign Language. *Language and Speech*, 42(2-3):143–176.

Nespor, M. and Vogel, I. (1986). *Prosodic Phonology*. Mouton de Gruyter, Berlin.

Ormel, E. and Crasborn, O. (2012). Prosodic Correlates of Sentences in Signed Languages: A Literature Review and Suggestions for New Types of Studies. *Sign Language Studies*, 12(2):279–315.

Prillwitz, S. (1989). *HamNoSys Version 2.0. Hamburg Notation System for Sign Languages: An Introductory Guide*. Intern. Arb. z. Gebärdensprache u. Kommunik. Signum Press.

Selkirk, E. (1984). *Phonology and syntax. The relation between sound and structure*. MIT Press, Cambridge, Mass.

Stokoe, W. (1960). Sign Language Structure: an outline of the Visual Communication Systems of the American Deaf. *Studies in linguistics: Occasional papers*, 8.

Stokoe, W. C. (1980). Sign Language Structure. *Annual Review of Anthropology*, 9(1):365–390.

Valin, R. D. V. (1993). A synopsis of Role and Reference Grammar. In Valin, R. D. V., editor, *Advances in Role and Reference Grammar*, page 30. John Benjamins Publishing Company.

Vermeerbergen, M. (2006). Past and current trends in sign language research. *Language & Communication*, 26(2):168–192. In: Language and Communication. (25 blz.).

Vermeerbergen, M., Leeson, L., and Crasborn, O. A. (2007). Simultaneity in Signed Languages.: A String of Sequentially Organised Issues. In Vermeerbergen, M., Leeson, L., and Crasborn, O. A., editors, *Current Issues in Linguistic Theory*, volume 281, pages 1–25. John Benjamins Publishing Company, Amsterdam.

Vermeerbergen, M. and Van Herreweghe, M. (2018). Looking back while moving forward: The impact of societal and technological developments on Flemish sign language lexicographic practices. *International Journal of Lexicography*, 31(2):167–195.

Yin, K., Moryossef, A., Hochgesang, J., Goldberg, Y., and Alikhani, M. (2021). Including Signed Languages in Natural Language Processing. *arXiv:2105.05222 [cs]*. arXiv: 2105.05222.

Zeshan, U. (2007). Towards a notion of 'word' in sign languages. In Dixon, R. and Aikenvald, A. Y., editors, *Word: A cross-linguistic typology*. Cambridge: Cambridge University Press.

Zhou, Z., Levin, L., Mortensen, D. R., and Waibel, A. (2020). Using Interlinear Glosses as Pivot in Low-Resource Multilingual Machine Translation. *arXiv:1911.02709 [cs]*. arXiv: 1911.02709.

Association for Computational Linguistics
209 N. Eighth Street
Stroudsburg, Pennsylvania 18360

ISBN 978-1-7138-3921-7

CURRAN ASSOCIATES INC.
proceedings.com